P9-CSV-983

ACKNOWLEDGMENTS

Although you must become captain of your own destiny—never forget to help those who built your boat or manned your oars.

Ever since I can remember, I've loved this great game and the people associated with it. My "dream" as a young boy was to one day become a professional golfer.

I have been fortunate to have played and taught in countries around the world. Along the way, there have been so many people who have helped shape and support my career.

My wife, Colleen, has been my greatest supporter. She's never complained no matter how many trips I've taken, or how many late nights or early mornings were spent working, or how many times requests for my help have taken me away from our time together. She is truly my partner in life.

To my father, Warren, my mother, Edie, and my two brothers, Gary and Richard, thanks for all your help and support.

Many of my students have become close friends as well as business associates. Their time, knowledge, and expertise have been instrumental in my development as a person and as a businessman. To Al and Lucille Omson, my friends and advisors: thank you for always being there to guide me.

To Richard "Skip" Bronson, Gary Leeds, Dan Epstein, Tony McLaughlin, thanks for your advice, support, and friendship, and a very special thanks to Steve Wynn.

I would also like to thank some very important people for their help in the preparation of this book:

To Ken Van Kampen, for his dedication and writing skills in bringing my thoughts to the printed word. Darrel Millsap (illustrations) and Karla M. Roberts (character illustrations), your artistic and creative illustrations brought life to my images. Thank you for your dedication to this project.

To Warner Depuy, Jib Colthsworthy, and Signature Sports, along with John Delehanty, Mitch Rogatz, Siobhan Drummond, and Triumph Books, thank you for your help and your belief in making this happen.

Thanks to Gary Reinmuth, whose editing and writing skill brought clarity and interest to the text of this book.

To Bob Kwait, a creative genius, whose talent has produced so many of the my marketing and design masterpieces, you were there in the very beginning of my teaching career. Thanks for all your help and talent.

And finally, to my friend Bob Toski, for giving me a priceless gift—your time, knowledge and support, for which I am truly thankful.

True success is helping others become successful. To all those who have helped me, thank you.

Live your dreams,
Dean Reinmuth

CONTENTS

FOREWORD

It is with great pleasure that I write the Foreword for the excellent instructional book written by my friend, Dean Reinmuth.

I first met Dean Reinmuth when he came to me for instruction regarding his golf swing as a tour player. Since that time, I have watched him grow as a teacher and professional in this great game. In this day and time, when there are so many different theories on how to swing a golf club, it is refreshing to know that Dean has such a sound grasp on the fundamentals of the golf swing and how it should be taught and learned.

This is evident by the success he has had with Phil Mickelson, who is destined for stardom on the PGA Tour. What impressed me the most is how well he has handled Phil's transition from the amateur ranks into the professional field. Dean's wisdom and knowledge prove to me the great qualities he has to teach people how to grow and mature in such a competitive world.

He deserves all the success he can get and I wish him all the best.

Bob Toski

INTRODUCTION

WHAT I TEACH THAT'S DIFFERENT

My teaching method is probably very different from anything you've encountered before. Most instructors teach the importance of copying a specific mechanical plan from the start of the swing to its finish. I believe it's far more important to focus on the *motion* of the swing. Motion is destroyed by tension, so I also teach the importance of locating tension and eliminating it, helping you swing the club on a more consistent path and with greater speed. I teach my students they should be able to swing as effortlessly at the ball as they do when they make a practice swing, without tightening, flinching or guiding. I also teach how to shape the swing correctly, what I call form, by watching your reflection and using the clubhead to find proper swing positions. Finally, I teach my students how and on what to focus and how to practice so that they can maintain the freedom of motion and sound swing form they've found. Once my students have succeeded at learning these things, they find that they are, indeed, hitting their best shots more often.

FORMULATING MY INSTRUCTIONAL APPROACH

In order to understand better how my swing-shaping system can help you teach yourself how to improve your game, it's important for you to understand how my background and experiences formulated my approach to teaching.

I've been hooked on golf ever since my father first asked me to caddy for him when I was a five-year-old growing up in Downers Grove, Illinois. It wasn't long after that I was using Dad's clubs to practice pitching, chip-

Me and my father, Warren, who introduced me to the game of golf when I was two.

ping and putting. I sunk some Campbell's soup cans in the yard and built myself a little course. I'd spend hours hitting plastic golf balls around the house, over the vegetable garden and into the sand box. It was my own championship track and I created new holes every day.

A few years later I started caddying at a local course, Naperville Country Club, a couple of times a week in order to make some extra money and play for free on Mondays, which was caddy day. When I was about thirteen, I started working as a greenskeeper at Downers Grove Golf Club, a nine-hole public course. The pay was low, but employees were allowed to play as much golf as we wanted for free during our off-hours, and that was what counted most to me. After that I was hired as the starter and assisted in the pro shop at Woodridge Golf Club, with the same provision of free golf. I played as much as I possibly could during the warm weather, and when winter came and the course closed, I'd clear snow from patches of ground in the backyard so I could hit pitch shots. I also practiced chipping and putting in my bedroom in order to make it through till spring.

In the early '60s there wasn't nearly as much golf instructional material available as there is today. Most people were left to figure out how to swing on their own.

"Caddy swings" were the norm — unorthodox styles that people figured out for themselves. I tried to pattern my own swing after my idols, Byron Nelson and Ben Hogan and later Tom Weiskopf, who was tall like I was. I'd spend hours practicing, watching my reflection in the picture window of our house. But although I tried to copy the good swings of other players, I was never completely sure that I was doing it right, a feeling I think many golfers are familiar with. Eventually I grew frustrated with my own lack of knowledge. I just wasn't sure what I was doing. Still, I managed to muddle through fairly well on my own and, after shooting even par for the first time when I was fourteen, I decided that someday I was going to turn professional.

About a year after that I had my first formal lesson with a local teaching professional. Unfortunately, it did little to help me understand either how my swing worked or what made a good swing happen. I signed up for the lesson because I was duckhooking my drives sporadically. That, in turn, was wreaking havoc with my confidence and my ability to play solid competitive golf. To my disappointment, the professional told me that, in order to cure my duckhooking, I should slow my swing down. My reaction to his advice was to ask, "How can I hit the ball a reasonable distance if I slow my swing down?" He told me I was going to have to be willing to sacrifice some yardage to gain more control over my driver. Although I felt that might be true, I was sure there had to be a way to stop duck-hooking *without* giving up any clubhead speed. I had heard that Ben Hogan had once had the same problem and had cured it without slowing his swing down. I knew there must be a way for me to do the same, although I didn't have a clue how.

Despite an occasional duckhook I played well enough in high school to make the varsity team four years in a row at Downers Grove North, where I won an Illinois High School Association District Golf Championship as a sophomore. After graduation I attended Western Illinois University in Macomb, Illinois, on a golf scholarship.

Through it all, my game remained "okay," but I knew I had the potential to improve and was frustrated by my inability to reach the next level.

I still didn't feel as if I understood my swing very well. I continued to be haunted by the occasional duckhook, but only when I played in competition. During practice, it would disappear. I sought professional help to solve the problem, but whenever I took a lesson, the problem wouldn't occur. Still, I got plenty of advice.

First, I was told I should swing into a "reverse C" position at the finish. Next, I was told I should keep my right knee kicked inward as I swung (I was told to practice this by placing three balls under the outside of my right foot). Then someone informed me I had to keep my right arm close to my body during the downswing. I tried out different instructors, tips and even friends. (You know, the "Helpful Henrys" who are always trying to set you straight. They mean well, but aren't qualified to teach. Still, we listen.)

Every time I added a new swing tip or key to my list I ended up playing worse. That's something I think most of us can relate to. Eventually, I went back to working completely on my own, still hitting the occasional tournament duckhook.

The turning point came when I became convinced that Bob Toski, the chief instructor for *Golf Digest* at the time, had an approach that would help me. It struck me that many of the things I felt about the swing were echoed in the things Toski was saying in print. I decided that since he was the best, he was the instructor I wanted to learn from.

HELPFUL HENRY

Be careful and avoid the tendency to listen to all the helpful tips.
Keep your swing simple.

In the summer of 1973 I tracked down his phone number, and although I didn't know him and he certainly didn't know who I was, I called him to ask for help. He was extremely congenial and invited me to come down to see him. When I hinted that my finances might not allow that right away, he "ordered me" not to worry about the money and set me up with a free hotel room. So off I went to spend a week in Florida.

Working with Bob turned out to be one of the greatest experiences of my life. He was able to give me a clear and logical understanding of all the things that combined to make the golf swing work, and how any person can learn to make a better swing and come closer to reaching his or her potential in both distance and accuracy. For the first time, I felt as if there was light at the end of a long, dark tunnel. I suddenly had a direction to move in, a path to follow.

**I first sought out Bob Toski for his teaching expertise,
which turned out to be the beginning of a long friendship.
Above, when we first met, with Bob Rogers.**

Bob Toski and me, teaching in Japan.

Bob also showed me that I had a few bad habits that were going to take some time and effort to break. That's when it occurred to me that although Bob could help me understand what I needed to do physically to make a better swing, it was up to me to train my body how to do it. That was a very important realization. I recognized that even if I consciously knew I needed to make a swing change, just knowing it in my head didn't mean my body was going to perform it.

Another thing that impressed me about Toski, besides his overall knowledge of golf, was the way he went about teaching. Although I had already had some experience giving lessons while working as an assistant pro, they too often ended up as nonproductive half-hours. But Bob approached teaching with so much enthusiasm that his students couldn't help but get enthused themselves. He seemed to give people confidence they could become better players just because he fervently believed they could, and he genuinely had fun while doing it. I had never seen that kind of spirit in teaching golf before, and it made a strong impression on me.

When the time came to leave, I asked Bob if there wasn't something I could give him for all his help, but he told me not to worry about it. "You can pay me back when you win the U.S. Open," he told me.

Although I never got that far, I hope I've been able to give something back to him for all he has given to me, not just that week but over the years, for which I'm truly thankful. We've since remained good friends, and I have taught with him many times in Japan.

Back home in San Diego I went to work learning the things Bob had taught me. Although I didn't get better overnight, I knew the information I had been given was sound, and I gradually started to see improvement, which was encouraging.

But although I was swinging and striking the ball better, I still wasn't having much luck at handling my nerves during competition. It was obvious to me that my inability to focus properly was interfering with my physical ability to perform, but I didn't know how to remedy the situation. I confided in my sponsor, Bill Miller, about my concerns, and he convinced me to do some reading about the powers of positive thinking.

I was willing to try anything, so I followed his advice and read anything about the subject I could get my hands on. I was intrigued by the idea that the way a person thought — their mental processes — played such a powerful role in how they performed physically. However, I knew that whenever I had tried to think "positive thoughts" in the past — i.e.,

Bob Toski and me today.

"Hit straight down the middle" or "You can sink this putt" — those thoughts never seemed to counteract a bad gut feeling.

For instance, whenever I experienced a deep-rooted feeling that I was going to hit a poor shot, no amount of "rah rah" talk in my head could overcome that feeling, and the resulting shot was almost always poor. I realized that kind of internal exchange happened to me a lot during competition. I'd say something to myself like: "Okay, Dean, make a good swing here and drive it right down the middle." Meanwhile, my gut feeling would overwhelm me with the notion that I was going to make a quick, jerky swing, and that I'd hit a bad shot. Then, when I hit the ball, my gut feeling would win out and a big duck would come out to greet me.

All that brought me to the realization that my inability to focus properly was getting in the way of my improvement, and that I had to do something about it. So, in the fall of 1974 (which was well before "sports psychology" was in vogue), I attended a seminar on success motivation, which consisted of a series of lectures on how to convince yourself to do your best and also about how to focus better on achieving your goals through self-hypnosis (an idea which was about as popular and believable back then as the thought of going to the moon had been before it was actually done). I was hoping the seminar might be helpful to a golfer, and seeing Gene Littler in the audience reassured me.

The seminar convinced me it was possible for a person to learn to control his focus and gain more trust in his physical ability, that making mental improvements was just as important as making swing improvements.

In other words, I realized there are two sides to golf: the Technical Side and the Mental Side.

Although these two sides are separate, they directly affect each other, and when they work in harmony great golf is the result.

Great players like Hogan and Nicklaus are known not only for their ability to strike the ball, but also for their mental toughness.

Coming to that conclusion gave me a lot of hope. I continued to work at adopting Toski's advice and was seeing improvement, albeit slowly. That puzzled me — it was as if my head knew how to perform my new swing, but I couldn't force my body to do it. As I plugged away, I also tried to learn more about the mental side.

I signed up for a series of self-hypnosis seminars in San Diego with Bill and Carol Baras of the Baras Foundation, zeroing in on the aspects I thought would be beneficial to golf, particularly self-help, relaxation and hypnosis. Eventually, I actually became a certified hypnotist in the state of California.

While studying self-hypnosis I came across a study conducted by a major university with some of its basketball players. The players were divided into four groups. Each group was assigned a different practice regimen for free throws. Each group practiced its regimen for thirty days.

Group 1 was required to practice shooting free throws for two hours.

Group 2 was required to shoot free throws for one hour, then to imagine making free throws for an hour.

Group 3 was required to imagine making free throws for two hours.

Group 4 neither practiced shooting nor imagined making free throws.

The results? Not surprisingly, Group 1 finished first and Group 4 finished last. But what was interesting was that Group 3 beat Group 2, when no one in Group 3 had physically shot a free throw in thirty days. The study was a strong testament to the importance and power of the mind in regard to performing physical activities. Overall, the seminars I participated in helped me come to another very important realization, which was that in order to learn how to do a specific physical action, our minds must first grasp the concept of how to do it. Then, it's up to the mind to teach the body how to perform the action. For this process to occur properly and completely, learning has to take place slowly, and not be rushed. The way your body learns how to perform is through a **guided discovery approach** or, in other words, a form of trial and error (specific procedures will be outlined later).

I realized that was why it was taking me so long to break my bad habits and replace them with the good ones Bob had taught me — I had been expecting myself to perform new things too quickly and too perfectly. For example, one of the things Bob had told me was that my body was too fast at the top of my swing, and that I needed to both use less body and make a smoother motion. But I didn't know how much less and he couldn't tell me specifically, and that confused me. I knew I was wrong and I knew what I was supposed to do, but I couldn't do it. The solution came through a combination of things I had learned in the seminars, from Bob and from myself. I realized that by experimenting with different levels of speed and effort I should be able to come up with a combination that worked. So I went to the practice range, and using a simple scale of one to five — one being very slow and five being very fast — I set out to teach myself what my proper swing speed should be. Using the scale, I figured that my old speed rated about a four, which Bob had said was too fast. However, I knew that the slower swing speed I had been attempting to use didn't seem to be working either, and that rated about a two.

Therefore, it didn't take a rocket scientist to figure out that my ideal swing speed must rate about a three on the scale. (That was part of the beauty of it — it was so simple that I couldn't believe I hadn't thought about experimenting like this before whenever I'd had a problem). I tried hitting balls with the change and noticed a marked difference. Despite that, I still had a hard time trusting the change, because all along I, like a lot of golfers, had associated body effort with distance. Although my results were good and seeing was believing, I still found it hard to trust that an easy swing would allow me to get the kind of distance I needed.

Those conflicting feelings aside, I knew that I had discovered a valuable learning device, and decided to call it trapping, because I had trapped the right feeling in between the extremes of too much and too little. I got the idea from my friend and business advisor, Al Omson, who had related this type of process to me as it pertained to business and how to help determine what a good deal was. Later, I realized how well it could be used to make learning to determine that proper swing easier. (In Chapter 5 trapping will be explained in more detail.)

After that happened, it dawned on me that although a good teacher could diagnose a problem and guide a person in the right direction toward fixing it, it was up to the student to fine-tune the feeling and then recall the feeling when he needed it on the course. Before that, I had always expected the instructor to "quick fix" my swing problems and give me a specific cure. Instead, I came to the conclusion that it's essential for the student to assume an active, rather than passive, role in taking the information from the instructor and working with it to teach his body how to perform it correctly.

Ironically, just when all of these things started to click and come together in my head, I reached a crossroads in regard to my playing career. It became apparent that certain changes in my life would not allow me to continue with it, and although that was disappointing, I was excited by the idea that staying home in San Diego would allow me to further develop my theories and try to teach them to others. The more I thought about it, the more excited I got, because I really felt that the things I'd learned would allow me to take a much different approach to teaching, and I was anxious to see how it would work on all levels of players. So, armed with the same intensity I had applied to playing professionally, I set out to become one of the best teachers in the game.

TENSION: GOLF'S WORST ENEMY

I continued working on formulating my own teaching ideas based on my theories. In doing so, I actively observed as many different players as I could, and eventually I was struck by a big similarity between them: It seemed that the great majority of golfers, before hitting a ball, stand back and take a fairly smooth, easy, rhythmic practice swing, but then use a glaringly different swing when hitting the ball. Instead of being smooth and rhythmic, the "ball" swing was usually tight and jerky. It seemed that the simplest approach would be to take the practice swing, which was almost always good, and get them to use it over the ball.

It was pretty obvious to me that physical tension was what caused the change between the practice swing and the "ball" swing, and the result of that tension was a loss of clubhead speed and disturbance of the natural clubhead rotation and forward-swing path of the clubhead. In other words, tension was usually the cause of hitting short and/or crooked shots.

I came to believe that unwanted tension results in the manipulation of the clubhead instead of motion, which is the root of the great majority of ball-striking problems among players. Yet most players are oblivious to it, usually believing the problem is with some other technical part of their swing, when in fact the main problem is that they're too tense, which destroys their freedom of motion.

One gentleman who came to me (his nickname was "Señor Loopy") was typical: During our first lesson I asked him to hit a shot so I could make some observations. He took a club and first made a beautifully long, flowing practice swing, then rolled a ball into position and attacked it with a long, looping slash, hitting a low, ugly slice. After watching it, he turned to me and said he thought the problem had something to do with his grip position! His case clearly illustrates how the average player is far too concerned with technical adjustments, ball contact or shot results, when in fact the problem is that he has no freedom and motion in his swing. Not that technique isn't important, because it certainly is, and will be discussed later. However, technique doesn't have to be perfect — there is no perfect technique.

Look at great players and you'll see they have specific swing characteristics that distinguish each from the others. This is also true of the average player. It's clear that a golfer's biggest hurdle then is to rid his or her swing of tension and replace it with absolute freedom. It's basically a question of whether we find proper swing position through motion, or motion through proper swing position. I believe it's the former.

You find proper swing position through motion, because without motion, there is no swing.

Swinging without tension sounds easy, and it is. Most players usually demonstrate how easy when they make a practice swing. But when you step up to a ball, it's amazing how tense and jerky you can become — your focus usually changes from the swing motion to ball contact (what I call being "ball-focused"), resulting in tension. And it only takes a little tension — a lot of people can stay loose until a fraction of a second before impact, when they tighten up just a tiny bit — to ruin a shot.

I took my ideas and started to apply them to some golfers I was teaching at Stardust, and was delighted to find that several players made great progress in their games. Most were amazed at how the ball would seem to jump off the clubface with such little apparent effort once they got rid of their tension and started swinging freely. When that happened I knew that I had found my true calling in golf as a teacher, not only because my approach seemed to work so well, but also because I found it so gratifying to help people improve so much. Before, I had always found it rewarding whenever I could help a person get better at the game, but the results were so dramatic with my approach that it made teaching an even bigger thrill.

At that point, the only thing I wanted to do was teach, so I became a full-time instructor. I started teaching classes on the mental side of golf, as well as a special course for professionals, sort of an "instructor instruction" class. I continued this routine for eight years before starting my own golf school, which includes individual instruction, corporate golf programs and a professional development program designed to help promising players prepare to play professional golf.

I have kept in touch with Bob Toski, who has always wholeheartedly supported the direction my career has taken. It was through Bob's association with *Golf Digest* that, in the summer of 1983, I was asked to in-

Three-time NCAA Champion, winner of the 1990 U.S. Amateur and five PGA Tour events, Phil Mickelson and I have been working together since we met in 1983, when he was thirteen.

struct at one of *Golf Digest's* five-day junior schools held in Pinehurst, North Carolina. It was there that I met a thirteen-year-old named Phil Mickelson. It turned out he was also from the San Diego area and, coincidentally, he and his family were members at Stardust, so that gave us a lot to talk about. Phil mentioned that he had heard about my work from two touring professionals from San Diego, and asked if there was any possibility I could work with him when we got back.

We agreed to get together and talk about it, and after meeting with him and his parents I took him on as a regular student. It proved to be the beginning of a long teacher-player relationship.

Phil posted the best amateur/collegiate record since a guy named Nicklaus. To be able to have helped someone reach the level that Phil is at makes me all the more happy that I decided to become an instructor. But when I think back to when we first met, I had no idea at the time that he'd develop into such a fine golfer and good friend. But that's golf — the possibilities are endless.

1

THE ULTIMATE GOAL

There is one essential to the golf swing—the ball must be hit.
Sir Walter Simpson
Art of Golf (1887)

Everyone who has grown to love the game knows how difficult golf can sometimes be and how much frustration it can cause. I know, because I've been there. But think back for a minute how many times you've already made great swings, hit great shots or stroked great putts. Those instances prove you do possess a certain level of ability. The problem is most of us don't perform at that level often enough. So I'm going to open this book with two simple statements:

YOU can become a better golfer.

Hitting a golf ball consistently well is not as hard as YOU might think it is.

All golfers want to achieve two things: To improve the quality of our shots. And to reach a higher level of consistency, so we can hit our best shots more often. In trying to find solutions to these problems, the mind typically goes on a search mission, haphazardly testing an array of tips or technical swing changes without a plan or understanding of how the movements of the swing fit together correctly. This usually results in frustration and little improvement.

I am absolutely convinced a good golf swing is an acquired skill and can be learned in the same way you learned to walk, speak and write. Such learning will occur in gradual stages of development — not overnight. But it will happen, and you can do it, if you are given good information and if you approach the learning one step at a time.

Every player's ultimate goal should be:

To hit his best shots more often, while hitting fewer bad shots.

When I say bad shots, I mean the really awful ones, the clunkers that come out of nowhere. Part of your goal should be to reach a level where your worst shots still turn out playable. Someone once said, "It's not how many great shots you hit during a round of golf, but how few bad ones." I agree completely. The key to good scoring isn't usually how many great shots you hit in the course of eighteen holes, but how acceptable your bad ones are.

The chief reason most golfers don't play up to their potential and hit more good shots is because they suffer from too much tension. Tension is the biggest roadblock there is to making a good swing. Physical tension reduces clubhead speed and prevents the clubhead from swinging freely and returning the clubface through the ball squarely. Mental tension clouds your ability to focus clearly and swing freely.

Tension also causes inconsistency. Sound familiar? Every golfer knows what it's like to hit a poor shot and then follow it with a great shot. Confused, we wonder why we can't hit all our shots well. The fact is, no one can. A lot of people seem to think the ultimate goal in golf is to hit the ball perfectly with every swing; but I disagree, not because it isn't a nice idea, but simply because it's downright unattainable. Striking a golf ball flawlessly requires too much precision — remember, we're human beings, not robots.

I've written this book because I've developed a system I believe will enable any player to rid himself of tension and improve the overall quality of his shots (longer and straighter), and to hit his best shots more often while hitting fewer bad shots.

My system is based on sharpening the technical side of your game. It enables you to make a more efficient, effective swing and improve your focus. That, in turn, will help develop trust in your swing feelings and emotions. Your mind and body will then be working together when you swing, instead of against each other.

I've been using this method for over fifteen years and have applied it to thousands of players of all handicaps and seen the exciting results. In fact, I've watched absolute beginners go from learning how to grip the club to hitting acceptable shots within the course of one day.

To achieve results, you, the reader, must make a commitment. What follows in these chapters is all the information I've garnered in my more than thirty years as a player, student and teacher of the game.

Don't worry; my plan is very simple and it won't take long. Just stay on the path and follow the directions, and you'll eventually be hitting the ball in real life as well as you do in your daydreams.

2

MAKING LEARNING EASY

If they taught sex like they teach golf, the human population would have died out centuries ago.

Jim Murray
Los Angeles *Times*

The ability to play golf is an acquired skill. Believe it or not, there was once a time when Jack Nicklaus didn't know anything about the game, a time before Luciano Pavarotti knew what opera was or Julia Child had any inkling of how to cook. That's not to say all of these people didn't have certain innate abilities that allowed them to excel in their given fields, but in the beginning they had to learn the basics of their professions just like everyone else.

So whether you're a beginner or an experienced player who wants to improve, rest assured you *can* reach your goal; but first, you must improve your ability to learn and to teach yourself.

When it comes to learning, you have two choices: the easy road or the hard one. If your choice is the easy one, read on about how we learn, and ways we can enhance learning rather than hinder it.

TWO LEVELS OF THE BRAIN: ANALYTICAL AND PERFORMANCE

I made two very important discoveries on my journey to becoming a better teacher. First, I realized it was not only my role to impart good swing information to my students, but also to teach them how to experiment properly with the information they had been given so they could, in effect, teach themselves what was correct, and how to find it again if they lost it. Second, I realized that when an individual experiences a problem with his swing, it is important he be able to assess the cause in order to fix it.

In researching the brain's abilities to learn, I discovered there are two basic levels of the brain: the analytical level and performance level. The analytical level is where you think, analyze, criticize and make decisions. In deciding what club to hit — taking into account the distance, the lie, the wind, etc. — you're using the analytical level of your brain. When you tell yourself to do something — "Keep your head down!" — you're also functioning on the analytical level.

ANALYTICAL VS. PERFORMANCE

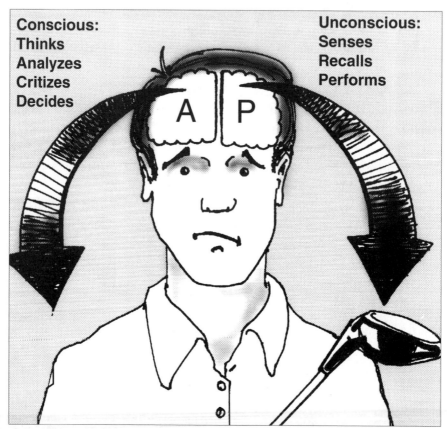

Conscious:
Thinks
Analyzes
Critizes
Decides

Unconscious:
Senses
Recalls
Performs

Don't be confused . . . it's easier than you think. There are two levels of the brain: analytical, which consciously thinks, analyzes, criticizes and decides; and performance, which unconsciously senses, recalls and performs. The golf swing works best when executed on the performance level.

The performance level is responsible for actions we do without thinking about them. When you sense, recall or perform something based on what you feel without consciously thinking about it, you're using the performance level of the brain.

I like to refer to the analytical level as the "teacher," because it is responsible for taking information and conveying it to the performance level, which I refer to as the "player."

However, just having information on the analytical level doesn't mean you'll be able to automatically apply it to the performance level. Simply giving yourself verbal directives ("swing smooth," "hit down") does not guarantee your body will be able to respond.

For example, suppose someone who knows nothing about golf reads a book all about the swing. When he's finished, he understands what he's supposed to do in order to hit a golf ball. He knows he should grip the club a certain way and assume a certain posture, etc. Does that mean he'll be able to go to the golf course and shoot 70? Of course not, because although he understands what to do on an analytical level, he hasn't had a chance to teach that information to his performance level. That's also why, as an instructor, I teach you how to feel your swing. I'll give you good information and train you to experience the sensations so you can take information from your analytical level and teach it directly to your performance level. If it makes sense to you, you can more easily make the needed change.

However, don't expect that your "player" level will immediately be able to catch on to everything your "teacher" level has to impart to it. In other words, just because your mind understands what to do, it doesn't mean your body will be able to perform it right away. You need to be familiar with the feeling of a good swing in order to perform one. This is the major difference between *thinking* about the swing and *feeling* it. You can't simply take swing information and immediately transmit it to the performance level. The proper swing is acquired over time with proper repetition, just like learning how to walk or write.

Eventually, when the performance level of your brain grasps the feeling, it holds on firmly, as in the old saying . . . "it's like riding a bike; once you learn how, you never forget." Think back to when you first started learning to drive and you had to consciously think about every move you made — fasten your seat belt, put the key in the ignition, start the car, put your foot on the brake, shift the car into gear, etc. But after you'd

ACQUIRING INFORMATION ANALYTICALLY

In order to teach your body how to perform something, you must first acquire the information on an analytical level. A little info goes a long way; don't overdo it.

been driving for a while you reached the point where you could jump in and run through all those actions without giving them hardly a thought. That's because you had learned how to execute them at the performance level. Once that occurred, your performance level didn't need any help from your analytical level.

That's your goal with the golf swing: to perform it without having to consciously direct it. Don't forget, though, that the performance level needs time to acquire this skill.

Remember, anything worth learning will take a certain investment of your time and effort, but it will be well worth it.

PLAN YOUR PRACTICE

After you have acquired the information on the analytical level, your analytical level (teacher) must teach it to your performance level (player).

PRACTICE YOUR PLAN PATIENTLY

Once your performance level has learned the information from your analytical level, then both your body and mind will know how to perform the given task.

Level 1. Unconsciously Competent

Level 2. Consciously Compentent

Level 3. Consciously Incompetent

Level 4. Unconsciously Incompetent

There are four levels we go through to acquire any skill. Each
one takes time and slow practice before achieving the next level.

LEARNING IS A STEP-BY-STEP PROCESS

The problem with most golfers is that they want to learn golf too quickly.
They end up interfering with the learning process by trying to hurry it.
They don't follow an organized plan for improvement, spend very little
time practicing, yet they expect to immediately go out on the course and
lower their score.

When they perform more poorly than expected, they get frustrated
with the whole process. Bear in mind that acquiring any kind of skill involves some fumbling, and that mistakes will be made. Failure is a natural
part of the learning process.

Try this exercise. It's crucial to helping you understand the concept of
acquired skills and gradual learning. (Perform each step, one at a time,
before reading any further.) Above, you'll see my signature in four different forms next to four blank lines. First, write your signature quickly on

the first blank line, as if you were signing a check. Second, sign your name again on the next line, but very slowly, while trying to make an *exact* copy of the first, right down to the size, sweep and loop of each letter. Third, take the pen in your opposite hand and try to duplicate the basic form of your original signature on the third line. Finally, with the pen in your opposite hand, try to write your name on the fourth line as quickly as you did when making the first signature (don't worry about what it looks like).

Look at what you've done. Of the four lines, the first one probably looks the best — smooth and free-flowing — performed without conscious thought. There, you were unconsciously competent, which is the level you want to reach when you swing.

The second line probably looks okay, but the pen strokes lack freedom and smoothness because you were trying to be perfect and ended up "overcontrolling" the pen to avoid making a mistake. This is known as being consciously competent. Most players swing this way. They try to guide the clubhead to the ball, especially under pressure, instead of swinging it freely. This is probably similar to how you feel when you try to hit the ball to a well-guarded target or when there is pressure on you to play well — you focus most on trying to make perfect swings so as not to hit any errant shots.

The third line is probably pretty rough, though there might be some resemblances to the first two. On the third, you were consciously incompetent: Your mind understood what had to be done, but you haven't acquired the movement skill with your opposite hand to do so. You most likely wrote slowly so your mind and body could coordinate with each other to produce the letters properly. This is how you should proceed when learning the form of the swing.

The fourth line is most likely pretty messy. Here, you were unconsciously incompetent: You rushed headlong into signing quickly, but there was no skill, form or control to back it up. To sign your name quickly and legibly with your opposite hand, you would first have to learn to form the letters slowly, and then gradually pick up speed — the same way you learned with the hand you normally write with.

One of the main reasons we flounder so much at learning is because we all begin unconsciously incompetent. Instead of developing the feel and form of the swing gradually, we rush through learning, anxious to be able to play, which almost always results in poor results and slow progress. Everyone has the potential to perform better, but it's important to be patient.

MISTAKES: A PART OF LEARNING

Most of us aren't comfortable making mistakes. We don't want to embarrass ourselves. Instead, we should take a lesson from children. A child will implore someone to "watch me!" as he tries to hit a shot. He might mishit five in a row before finally succeeding on the sixth. Instead of fretting over a bad shot, he beams with pride over a good one. Learning is a process of continuing advancement through slow improvement. If the same analogy is applied to golf, it means we have to build success patterns with short, simple putts and chips before we try to rip a 250-yard drive.

You'll achieve your greatest improvements when you take your time and move along one step at a time. Don't proceed to the next step until you're sure you've mastered the one you're on.

This will take discipline and patience. It's natural to want to rush your progress, to move faster once you achieve a little success, but I assure you you'll get better results in the long run if you move slowly.

It's also important to approach learning with a relaxed attitude. Don't try to force progress. You'll find the harder you press, the more difficult progress becomes. That's not to say you shouldn't be dedicated to learning, but it should be a pleasurable experience. I've found that most people learn more quickly and keep their frustration at a minimum by dividing their practice time into short, frequent sessions rather than fewer, longer ones.

3

THE TWO SIDES OF GOLF:

TECHNICAL AND EMOTIONAL

If I had Jack's mind with my swing, you might never have heard of Nicklaus.

Tom Weiskopf
Golf Magazine

Early in my professional playing career, when I was bouncing between playing competitively and teaching, I made some interesting comparisons between myself and some of the less skilled golfers I taught. I was an experienced player who knew what was required to strike a golf ball well. I could execute the proper swing motion consistently, allowing me to hit five iron after five iron on the range and rarely land the ball outside twenty feet of my target. Despite this consistency, I was prone to hitting poor approach shots during competition, especially when I needed to hit it close.

I compared myself to a typical high-handicapper who has some major swing flaws. He's prone to missing his target area, too, even when hitting on the range, not so much because of nervousness, but because his swing isn't as sound as it should be.

I came to recognize that every golfer has two distinct sides, or facets—the technical side and the emotional side.

The technical side is your knowledge of the hows and whats of the golf swing. A good player knows not only how to swing but how to make an adjustment when something gets out of whack. He also knows how to hit different kinds of shots — long, short, high, low, left-to-right and right-to-left.

The emotional side involves how you feel about a certain shot before you hit it and whether those feelings are beneficial or detrimental to your ability to successfully focus and execute.

The technical and emotional sides are separate but they must work in harmony for us to play our best golf. For example, if Player A has a technically sound swing, but has a tendency under pressure to try to guide the clubhead, that means his emotional side lacks the proper focus or trust.

This will adversely affect his technical ability to hit the ball. If Player A is to fulfill his potential, learning to manage his emotional side will free up his already established technical abilities.

Player B may not display much knowledge of technique, but he has firm control of his emotional side. Player B isn't a good player because of his technical shortcomings, but he gets the most out of his physical ability because he doesn't handicap his performance mentally. For Player B to get better, he will have to work on improving his technical ability to make a better swing. (Note that this is just a hypothetical example. The fact is any player who lacks good technique will eventually experience emotional interference as well.)

THINKING VS. FEELING

Although good technical knowledge is important to developing and maintaining a sound swing, I want to make it clear that when it comes to hitting a golf ball well, you have to swing as you feel, not as you think.

Most golfers think instead of feel when they swing, and that's wrong. If I ask a student what his mind was focused on during his swing, he'll typically answer "I was thinking about turning my hips" or "I was trying to keep my right knee braced" or some other position-oriented thought. Even if these thoughts are technically correct, it is still very difficult to make a smooth, flowing swing unless your mind is focused on *feelings*.

Thinking and feeling are vastly different. Webster defines thinking as "to revolve ideas in the mind . . . to have the mind occupied on some subject . . . to deliberate, to consider or to judge." In contrast, feeling is defined as "to experience or perceive by touch or by contact . . . to perceive or be aware of by physical sensation."

Although technical knowledge is essential, never lose sight of the fact that, first and foremost, you must feel the swing and be aware of the sensation of it. You've probably had the experience of feeling you were going to hit a shot well. After you indeed hit it well you probably said to yourself, "I knew I was going to hit a good shot — I could feel it!"

I teach people to feel the swing instead of think about it, because you'll have much more success with feelings than with thoughts.

EMOTIONS: TRUST VS. DOUBT

Either you trust in your ability to make a good swing and hit a good shot or you don't. The greater your trust, the greater your odds of making a good swing, because you'll be able to focus on the shot better. By contrast, your odds of making a good swing decrease the more you doubt yourself. Doubt will distract you mentally, interfering with your ability to focus on the swing feeling you want. This produces mental tension or confusion which, in turn, creates physical tension, inhibiting your ability to make a good swing.

In order to trust yourself, you first need to develop a technically sound swing — not perfect, but capable. You can't trust to drive the ball accurately in the fairway if you don't possess the technique to do so. On the other hand, if your swing is technically poor and produces a lot of poor shots, then you'll be a lot more likely to doubt yourself when you step up to a ball.

TENSION: THE NUMBER ONE ROADBLOCK

Simply being technically correct doesn't mean you'll be able to perform well all the time, because your emotional side (trust/focus), which must work in harmony with your technical side, is easily affected by your playing circumstances. This is where things get interesting, because trust can easily be changed to doubt, and doubt creates tension, which is the worst enemy a golfer can have. Mental tension causes physical tension, which will prevent you from swinging the club with the maximum free-flowing motion you are capable of, while also preventing you from swinging it on a good forward-swing path, causing a loss of both distance and accuracy. Tension also will adversely affect your ability to perform shots you would normally be able to execute with ease.

This is what is commonly known as "choking." Imagine you had a three-foot putt to win your match or shoot your lowest round. If you had the same putt on the practice green, you would trust implicitly in your ability to make a smooth stroke and roll the ball in. With a match or a good score riding on it, that simple stroke becomes a lot more difficult. You start wondering if you can make it, rather than trusting the feeling of your stroke. Your hands and forearms tighten and you try to guide the ball into the hole, which changes your stroke and causes you to miss the putt.

PRACTICE SWING

Most golfers are ball bound. Tension isn't usually a problem during the practice swing.

BALL SWING

Yet most people tend to "chicken out" and tense up at some point when they swing at a ball. Their focus changes from swing to impact.

There are a lot of things that can undermine trust and cause tension. The target you're hitting to may be well-guarded or the lie may be difficult. You may need to hit a good shot to save par and win the match. You may face a long carry over water and know that you have to hit it perfectly to get over. You might be concerned about impressing your playing partner. There are lots of factors that can lead to tension, and they will vary according to each individual's strengths and weaknesses and what's important to them.

For example, two co-workers may tee it up with their boss one day. One is tense because he wants to play well in front of the "big guy." Meanwhile his friend is calm because he couldn't care less what the boss thinks. If I had to bet on who would play better, I'd pick the second guy.

Your current abilities are also important in determining whether you feel tension. Remember, it's doubt that causes tension, and the less you doubt yourself in a given situation, the less tension you'll feel. Imagine you've just putted a forty-footer that has cozied itself up to a few inches from the cup. Do you feel tense? No, because you've just hit a good putt and you have absolute trust in your ability to convert the tap-in.

Now, change that scenario a little so that instead of stopping near the cup, the first putt slides four or five feet past. That changes things, and you'll probably feel a twinge of doubt in your stomach because you didn't leave yourself with a gimme, and you know that if you miss it coming back you'll three-putt. All those thoughts lead to a lack of trust in yourself, which leads to tension when it comes to stroking that next putt. The more you trust in your ability, the easier the shot will seem.

For example, back in the days when Arnold Palmer was on top of the game, he used to take the old saying "never up, never in" to heart by almost always charging the ball three, four or five feet past the cup when he missed. When asked why he chose this strategy over a more conservative one, especially when it left him with so many knee-knocking second putts, he answered, "Because I was always so sure I could make the putt coming back if I missed the first one." He wasn't tense at all about stepping up to a lengthy little comebacker because he was so sure he could make it. Now, that's trust!

Some people have personalities that are naturally pretty good at keeping their emotional side under control. Historically, the greatest in the game are known for coming through in big tournaments, players like Palmer and also Nicklaus, Hogan, Trevino, Watson and Floyd. Such com-

One of your main priorities should be to eliminate tension from both your mind and your body.

petitors are commonly referred to as being "mentally tough" because they don't seem to allow any "outside influences" to affect their performance as much as others do. They control their emotions better, allowing them to fluctuate less, and that allows them to focus on performing. Amateurs, in contrast, allow their emotions to drift all over the place, especially by getting down on themselves.

But just as you can learn to sharpen the technical side of your game, you can also learn to control your emotional side. Take Watson from the above list: He was labeled a "choker" by some people for a while after twice losing leads in major tournaments. However, he eventually rose above that title to win eight majors, including five British Opens. It's not always a matter of whether "you've got it" or "you don't," but whether you're willing to work at developing your emotional control. The first step is to understand that your emotions, chiefly trust and doubt, play a key role in determining the existence of tension, and tension is detrimental to performance.

4

LEARNING VS. SURVIVING

---

*Golf is more how you learn than
what you know.*

Dean Reinmuth

One of the keys to eliminating tension is to avoid situations that cause doubt and instead seek out situations where you feel comfortable, relaxed and calm. When you're calm, you're able to focus better on what you're doing without worry or fear of failure or embarrassment. When you're calm you're more willing to take risks and experiment, both of which are important to your ability to learn and become aware of what good swings feel like. If you are in a situation where you feel cautious and tense because the shot is difficult or the circumstance causes pressure, you probably won't perform well because you'll just be trying to survive with whatever skills you've already developed instead of focusing on making good swings.

LEARNING SITUATIONS AND SURVIVAL SITUATIONS

You've probably experienced times when you feel tentative, nervous or unsure about performing even the simplest of tasks. It's not the task that creates your nervousness. It's the situation in which you're trying to perform.

Consider a beginner at basketball who's practicing shots alone. He's missing more than he's making, but he doesn't feel nervous because there's no pressure to make each one. If he misses, there's no penalty involved. He can simply take another shot and try to do better. Because he's calm he's free to focus on the things he needs to do to execute a good shot and build trust in himself. Given this kind of low-pressure situation,

LEARNING SITUATION

A learning situation is any situation where you feel relaxed and confident about performing.

he should see fairly rapid improvement. The more effectively a person is able to focus, the more quickly he will learn.

Now, take that same person and place him in a game situation with the score tied, one second left on the clock and a crowd of spectators making all kinds of noise. Chances are that he, a beginner, won't be calm at all or have much trust in his ability. When it comes to performing the shot, the poor fellow will probably be lucky to hit the rim, let alone make it.

The difference between these two situations is that the first one was a learning situation and the second was a survival situation.

SURVIVAL SITUATION

A survival situation is any situation where you feel tense and in-secure about performing.

A learning situation is any situation where you feel comfortable, calm and relaxed about either performing, practicing, experimenting or taking risks, where you aren't concerned about the consequences or failure. You feel this way because you hold a high degree of trust in your ability to perform the task or, even if you don't trust your ability, there's no pressure to perform it either perfectly or imperfectly.

A survival situation occurs any time you feel pressure to perform well, and that pressure creates doubt and tension which adversely affect your ability to learn or perform. In an instance like that you aren't able to focus well on performing, but instead are merely trying to survive. In a survival situation, your level of confidence will be low, your level of tension high.

Such feelings can spring from two sources. The first source is when there is pressure to perform well, but you lack the skill in the first place. In other words, you haven't developed the technical ability to perform what is required often enough to have confidence.

Imagine if you were asked to walk across a tightrope. Chances are you wouldn't want to try and, if you did, you'd certainly be extremely tense because you don't have the proper skills. Your lack of skill is the source of the tension.

A second source is when, despite the fact you possess the needed skills, the specific circumstances cause you to fear the consequences of failing. For example, imagine a long sidewalk, three feet wide. If you were asked to walk down it and not step off, you'd have no problem doing that. But suppose that sidewalk was suspended over the Grand Canyon. For most people, the act of walking on it would become impossible. The characteristics of the sidewalk haven't changed — it's still three feet wide. What has changed is the penalty for stepping off the edge! A highwire artist, on the other hand, might handle that situation with less worry because he or she has conquered the fear of heights and developed the special skills needed to succeed.

When it comes to doing anything, we all eventually reach a level where we no longer feel comfortable and where we begin to doubt our ability. Even a beginner will feel absolutely confident of his ability to sink a putt from a foot away; but as the ball is gradually moved farther from the cup, he will reach a point, maybe at two, three, four or five feet away, where he begins to lose his confidence.

It often takes only a slight shift in circumstances to change a learning situation to a survival one, and vice versa.

The practice tee is one of the most common learning situations in golf. There you are free to hit shot after shot without having to pay a penalty for bad ones. Your mind is free to focus on what you're doing. But what if Arnold Palmer happened by?

A former tour player and friend of mine was warming up his driver at a tournament, when suddenly out of the corner of his eye he noticed that Palmer had stopped right near him to do his own warming up. The last thing my friend wanted to do, of course, was hit a bad shot and embarrass himself. He had been hitting the ball perfectly up to that point. But the mere presence of Palmer changed the situation from a learning one to a survival one. My friend immediately put his driver away, took out a wedge, hit a few nervous shots, then left the range. This kind of thing has happened, in one form or another, to all of us. To conquer our fears and become better players, we have to learn to focus on our own swings and not on outside influences.

On-course circumstances determine whether you're in a learning situation or survival one. You may feel very comfortable playing a friendly match with friends, but very nervous when playing for your club championship. Most pros feel confident with a three-foot putt for par, but turn that three-footer into the difference between victory and defeat in the U.S. Open and it might cause a few butterflies in their stomachs.

Learning situations and survival situations vary from player to player, usually depending on their level of development. For example, skilled players usually view the course itself as a learning situation. They are confident in their abilities to hit fairways and greens and recover from the occasional poor shot. But that doesn't mean that during the course of a round they won't encounter some survival situations. Suppose a low-handicapper has only a mediocre sand game and finds his ball in a green-side bunker where he must explode onto a green that slopes away toward water. He probably won't feel too confident about that shot. He'll most likely be just trying to get onto the green without blading the ball into the water. Chances are good in fact that he'll overreact in the opposite direction and hit the ball too heavy, leaving it in the trap. Whether it's a tricky pitch shot, a long carry over water or a 10-foot putt to save par, such survival situations test the confidence of even the best players.

Less skilled players, meanwhile, usually view the entire course as a survival situation. The constant pressure to hit good shots, stay out of trouble and post a decent score can be upsetting. All that distracts them from playing their best and from learning.

CHANGING A SURVIVAL SITUATION INTO A LEARNING SITUATION

One of the main problems with trying to function in a survival situation is that learning occurs very slowly there, if at all. If you take a beginner and send him out on the course with good players at nine o'clock on a busy Saturday morning, he's going to be so nervous and self-conscious about performing that he's not going to be able to continue his learning during

PRACTICE TEE

In golf, the practice tee is a learning situation for most people . . .

the round, and it will probably turn out to be a bad experience. The idea that you'll be able to conquer your fears by continually confronting them at levels far above your ability level is wrong. Instead of learning, you'll end up relying on what you already know in a desperate attempt to survive. For example, I'm a novice skier who knows only a little about turning and stopping, and can only awkwardly snowplow. If I left the bunny hill and tried to ski down a difficult run, it wouldn't turn me into an expert. Instead, I would end up frantically relying on whatever skills I have already acquired — in other words, I would snowplow all the way down, trying hard not to fall and hurt myself.

As a matter of fact, when I took my first lesson I told my instructor I

FIRST TEE

. . . while the first tee is often a survival situation.

wanted to learn two things: how to stop so I wouldn't hurt myself, and how to turn so I wouldn't hurt anyone else. Unfortunately, even though I knew I had to stay relaxed I was stiff as a board.

Beginners need to seek out learning situations, because that's where they'll progress the fastest. Beginners should stick to the practice range or practice green until they've developed a certain amount of skill and trust.

When you start, make things as easy as possible on yourself by teeing the ball up, using a short-shafted club and making slow, short swings. And don't worry about either the distance or direction of your shot. Just try to make smooth, effortless swings.

When you think you're ready to play a course, you'll still most likely view it as a survival situation. What you want to do is turn the course from a survival situation into a learning situation. How? By eliminating the things that put pressure on you, like worrying about score. Unfortunately, everybody equates performance almost solely with score. And score, unfortunately, is not always the most accurate measure of how we have played.

My advice, to anyone who views the course as a survival situation, is to forget about score and simply try to make good swings. If you hit the ball into thick rough, move it out onto the short grass. If you're having trouble getting your fairway woods in the air, tee them up in the fairway. Hit a second ball whenever you feel like it. In other words, use the course as an upgraded driving range.

Sure, you're breaking the rules, but you're breaking them for the sake of learning, and that's okay as long as you aren't playing in competition or slowing down play. Doing these things will allow you to stay relaxed and confident on the course and help you learn more quickly to play different shots. It also will help if you choose an easy course — something that's flat and open.

Pick a time to play when there isn't a crowd, and hit off the short tees. Remember, you're trying to learn, not win a trophy, so make it easy on yourself and enjoy the experience. Instead of worrying about score, keep track of how many times you make a good swing without focusing on impact or trying to guide the clubhead.

Think of changing the course into a learning situation in terms of how a tightrope artist learns — not by first stepping out on the highwire, but instead by beginning on a wire that's close to the ground, gaining confidence there, then gradually raising the wire. What he's doing is controlling his learning environment, rather than allowing the environment to control him. If you resist this idea because you don't think it's "real golf," understand that the reason you do it is so that you can learn to play "real golf" better.

Be aware, though, that you can't baby yourself. You have to be willing to progressively increase the degree of difficulty. Your goal in making things easier first is to learn more quickly.

For example, if you've been removing the ball from bunkers because you aren't confident about your sand play, it's your responsibility to spend some practice time learning, so that eventually you can start hitting sand shots when you're on the course. It will help to look at difficult shots as a challenge to overcome, not as something to be afraid of. Not keeping score will make this easier.

How will you know when you've made the transition from a survival to a learning situation? A gut-check will tell you. If, when you step up to a shot, you feel nervous or very uncertain about your ability to play it, then it's a survival situation. You can only classify it as a learning situation if you no longer have continued feelings of uncertainty, frustration and fear of embarrassment. However, you don't have to be able to play a certain type of shot expertly every time in order to view something as a learning situation.

Someone who isn't yet proficient at playing bunker shots but who is confident they are on the right track and improving will view bunkers as a learning situation, even though they aren't great at playing out of them — yet. Once you have the confidence that you have the knowledge to play a shot and that you will be able to master it with practice, you're halfway to mastering it.

When you've reached a certain level of ability and can play a variety of shots with confidence, you'll feel more comfortable playing for score. When that happens, it means you've made the transition to viewing the course as a learning situation while playing for score.

5

TIPS FOR TEACHING YOURSELF

Laddie, you don't hit the ball on the backswing—you hit the ball on the forward swing.

Scottish caddie

I n the last chapter I talked about the importance of finding a place where you feel comfortable learning and performing. Now it's time to get on with that learning by exploring how to take the information I'm going to give you about the swing and teaching it to yourself in an efficient way. First, you'll need to get acquainted with two concepts that are crucial to your success in teaching yourself.

TRAPPING

Certain things about the golf swing are tough to convey with words. Take the forward-swing path of the clubhead: I can tell you it should approach the ball on a slightly inside-down-the-line-inside path, but I can't tell you what the exact path angle is or what it feels like. However, I can teach you that a way to find the proper path is to determine the two boundaries your goal lies between and experiment between those boundaries, gradually narrowing down what it is you're looking for until, bingo!, you've "trapped" the proper forward-swing path.

Your boundaries would be a sharply inside-out path and an outside-in path, knowing that somewhere in between is the ideal you're looking for. Using the accuracy of ball flight as your guide, you should experiment between those boundaries until you've narrowed things to a path that produces shots that start straight down the target line.

Trapping is useful in every aspect of the swing, from grip pressure to grip position to ball position, from posture to plane. When some aspect of your swing doesn't feel quite right, determine two boundaries and experiment within them until you trap the correct motion or feeling.

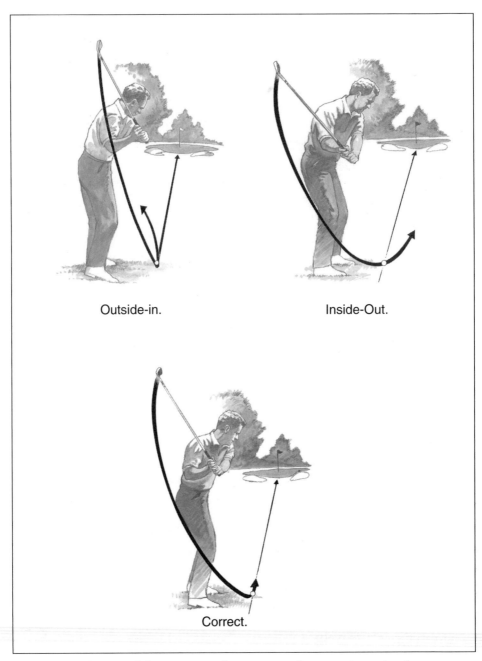

Outside-in.   Inside-Out.

Correct.

Trapping is the act of discovering what's correct by experimenting between two boundaries. Above, a perfect forward-swing path (middle) is "trapped" between one that's too far outside-in (left) and one that's too far inside-out (right).

Note that whenever you attempt to trap any of the major swing feelings described later in Chapter 10 you should assess each swing with gentle criticism and make gradual changes; your thought process should be something like "Not quite; almost; a little too much; still a little too much; aah, that's it!" It's important that you think positively instead of negatively — most people think in terms of "No, that's not it," when they should be thinking in terms of "Almost, close, perfect." Sometimes you need to use exaggerated feelings to get the proper results. One student described his new relaxed swing as spaghetti arms.

That's all there is to trapping. If it sounds simple, it's because it is (I told you in the beginning you didn't need to be a rocket scientist); but it's the single most important "skill" you'll need in order to teach yourself effectively and fix your swing when it needs adjustment. Of course, to successfully trap something, you have to have the technical knowledge of what to adjust and what the proper boundaries are.

The more you practice trapping, the better you'll become at doing it. Once that happens, you'll be amazed at the kind of control you can assume over your swing. Then, it's only a matter of how much time you want to spend at honing your swing that determines how much you improve.

THE "TRUST LADDER"

It's important when you're learning that you start at a level you can handle easily, where you trust yourself completely. I like to think in terms of what I call a "trust ladder," where performance on the lower rungs is easy but grows increasingly more difficult with each rung you climb.

For example, if I were instructing a player who was having trouble with long irons, I wouldn't send him out to practice his swing by hitting two irons off a tight lie. That level is too high on his trust ladder, and he's not ready to perform there. Instead, I'd tell him to start out with a short club he knew he could hit well, and have him place the ball up on a fluffy lie, and from there let him work his way up to tighter lies. Then he should move on to a slightly longer shaft and repeat the process, etc. Get the idea? When practicing, always start out at a level you've already mastered, which will put you in a positive, confident, trusting mood, keeping you relaxed and free of tension.

THE TRUST LADDER

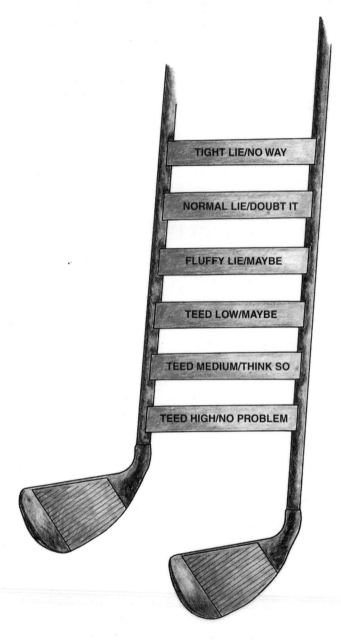

TIGHT LIE/NO WAY

NORMAL LIE/DOUBT IT

FLUFFY LIE/MAYBE

TEED LOW/MAYBE

TEED MEDIUM/THINK SO

TEED HIGH/NO PROBLEM

An example of a trust ladder: Steps to developing trust in your swing. Go slowly up each step; if you lose confidence, drop back down a step or two and keep yourself in a learning situation.

Generally, your level of trust will depend on the playing conditions (lie, wind, etc.), the club (some people lack trust in certain clubs), the presence of penalties for a poor shot (sand, water, etc.) and outside elements (competition, people watching, etc.). If something is causing you to doubt your ability, then you haven't mastered that particular trust level.

Trust levels in particular situations will vary from player to player. For example, low-handicappers, who already have a lot of developed skills, can usually start higher on the ladder, whereas high-handicappers will need to start lower. The low-handicapper may start practicing bunker shots by trying to get the ball within ten feet of the cup because he trusts that he can, and then begin working on gaining even more precision from that point. The high-handicapper, on the other hand, may want to start with simply attempting to get the ball out of the bunker, and then work toward putting the ball on the green, and so on. The idea is that each person must determine at what level he can trust his swing, and then gradually challenge himself with more difficult lies, smaller targets, longer putts, etc., in order to move up the trust ladder.

Recognizing where your position is on the trust ladder for a given situation and starting out at that level is important to how quickly your learning progresses. Whether you're working on your swing, sharpening your chipping or trying to learn to be a better putter, be honest with yourself. Don't be ashamed to humble yourself and start with the easiest conditions, because doing so will increase your odds of moving up the ladder more quickly. When I played competitively I was at a high level on the trust ladder when it came to iron play and chipping, but on a relatively low level when it came to my driver.

The most detrimental thing to effective practice is an exaggerated belief in how good you are. For instance, a golfer who has a hard time hitting the ball solidly isn't going to benefit much from working on shotmaking. He'll be a lot better off if he drops down a few levels on the trust ladder and goes to work on improving the technical side of his swing in order to make more consistent contact. Once he's done that, he can move up the ladder to the shotmaking level.

To determine whether you've mastered a certain level of trust, go with your gut feeling. Whenever I size up a shot, my feelings range from "No problem," to "I think so," to "I doubt it," to "No way." When you practice, start out with the shots that are "no problem," then move up to

TRUST LEVELS

	BEGINNER	INTERMEDIATE	ADVANCED
LIE			
DISTANCE CARRY			
DISTANCE LONG	Par 3	Par 4	Par 5
DIRECTION			
PUTTS	3 feet	15 feet	40 feet
CHIPPING			

Lack of trust at any of these stages will result in an overmanipulation or guiding feeling during the strike or swing. If you have difficulty in trusting, drip back to an easier level of shot.

BALL FOCUS — Tight Lie: The tendency is to focus on making solid contact.

IMPACT CLUBFACE SQUARE — Tight Fairway: The tendency is to try to square the face at impact.

CONTROL SPEED/DISTANCE — Proper distance tends to make us tighten our hands and forearm muscles to hold back the speed.

INCREASE SPEED — Extra Distance: Tends to make us "give it a little extra" creating a jerk or surge of speed.

Trust Levels

those that register an "I think so" until they, too, are "no problem," and so on.

If you have a desire to improve, which most people do, you won't be happy for long on a particular level of the ladder because once you attain something, it's natural to believe you can do better. If you're hitting one out of five fairways, and improve that to three out of five, you'll be satisfied for a while, but it won't be long until you'll want to hit four out of five. But remember, the best way to improve in any area of the game is to find a comfortable position on the trust ladder and work your way up from there. The key is to start with easy conditions: short putts, short chips, fluffy lies, large targets, and move "gradually" to more difficult ones.

TRY HARD, BUT NOT TOO HARD

I always try to impress on my students that discipline and determination are key elements to learning and improving. However, as with anything else, there exists a law of diminishing returns wherein the more you try, the less you'll get out of your efforts. In other words, if you try too hard, or "overtry," you'll end up putting pressure on yourself, which will hamper performance.

There's nothing wrong with determination — it's one of the greatest assets anyone can have. But you have to be able to recognize when it's working against you.

You'll often perform a lot better if you don't try so hard and don't worry so much about the outcome. Although it might sound ridiculous, you will actually trust yourself more when you don't care as much about what happens because you'll put less pressure on yourself.

Here's an example:

A friend and I were playing Augusta together. We didn't know much about the layout, but had been told to be wary of a particularly difficult par four on the back nine. It was long and narrow and had a tricky green. When we got to it, my friend, a middle-handicapper, hit a great drive, then followed it with a three-wood approach that finished ten feet below the hole — a fantastic shot.

Even though it was just a casual round and we weren't playing a match, he was still extremely excited by the prospect of making birdie on

Trying too hard often leads to tension and poor results . . .

the toughest hole on the course. It wasn't hard for me to guess what was going to happen next. He took a lot of time surveying the putt, which was uphill and broke slightly from right to left.

I could tell how badly he wanted to make it. But because of that, he tightened up and jabbed at the ball instead of stroking it, pulling it left of the cup and sending it four feet past the hole. That left him with a much more difficult putt than before, a slick downhill/sidehill slider.

In his disgust he took one brief look and smoothly drilled the ball into the back of the cup for par. On the next tee (after he'd had a chance to cool down), I asked if he'd realized how difficult his putt for par had been. Glancing back at the green, he said he guessed it was kind of tough, but that he hadn't really given it much thought.

. . . while trying less usually cultivates a more relaxed attitude and greater success.

"To tell you the truth," he replied, "after I'd blown the birdie putt, I didn't care that much whether I made par or bogey, so I didn't think much about the second stroke." Exactly, I told him, sometimes if you care too much, you perform worse than if you don't care that much. If he had approached the birdie putt with an attitude similar to the one he'd displayed toward the par putt, he would have had a better chance at making three.

You've probably experienced much the same kind of situation. It happens often when you're playing a practice round and are up against a difficult shot that you badly want to pull off. Your hands and arms tighten, causing a herky-jerky swing and a poor result. Then, with the pressure off, you drop a second ball for practice and, lo and behold, you make a smooth swing and hit a great shot. You didn't try as hard the second time, stayed relaxed, and those were the keys to your success.

I don't want you to get the idea I'm advocating a "don't-give-a-darn" attitude. What I am saying is to be on the lookout for situations where you might be tempted to try too much. Those are the times when trying less will yield better results.

6

HOW TENSION
DESTROYS THE SWING

---

*Too many golfers grip the club like
they were trying to choke a prairie
coyote to death.*

Curt Wilson,
Las Vegas Trick Shot Artist
Golf Digest (1970)

Before you embark on teaching yourself the swing, you need to determine what most likely is the matter with yours. Tension, as I have mentioned, is without question the biggest hindrance to playing golf well.

In my twenty years of teaching I have seen very few people whose swings weren't somehow negatively affected by tension. The fact is most golfers already realize that tension is a negative thing: Whenever I ask a student what his worst swings feel like, he'll usually say "jerky," "hard," or "a lot of effort." But when I ask what his best swing feels like, he'll usually say "smooth," "easy," or "effortless."

To me, a golfer saddled with tension isn't really swinging at all, but instead is manipulating or controlling the club at a cost of distance and accuracy. Tension primarily invades the fingers, wrists and forearms, but also may show up in the elbows, upper arms, shoulders, chest and back. When it occurs, it prevents the body from working smoothly and efficiently.

Tension can cause a wide range of swing problems, depending on how much tension there is and where and when it occurs. The most common problems it causes are poor clubhead speed, bad forward-swing path and faulty clubface alignment at impact.

Unfortunately, those who experience tension in their swings usually don't even realize it's there. And, if they do, they don't understand where it is, how much there is or how detrimental it is.

THE CURSE OF BRUTE FORCE

The No. 1 reason people get tense before swinging or at some point during their swing is because they focus on *killing the ball* and the *moment of impact* instead of the motion of the swing.

For some reason, when most golfers step up to swing at a golf ball, they believe it's going to take a great deal of physical effort on their part to hit it successfully. They tighten up the way they would if they had to move a heavy object. The famous golf instructor Ernest Jones called this "BF" for "brute force."

BF might be needed to make the slow, concentrated, "heave-ho" motion you'd use to move a piano, but you don't need it to swing a golf club. The object is to relax your muscles and get the clubhead moving fast and freely.

It's natural to equate the feeling of power with effort, and effort causes tension. But in golf, distance comes from clubhead speed and solid contact, clubhead speed comes from motion, and motion comes only when the muscles are relaxed. So, in fact, using less effort will equal more clubhead speed. Ever watch a professional hit a golf ball? If so, you've probably marveled at how effortlessly they appear to swing. That's not an optical illusion. The pro really isn't using much body effort to build a great deal of clubhead speed. By contrast, the typical amateur uses more effort (BF) but produces less speed.

The effect of tension on the forward swing is similar to slapping ankle weights on a sprinter. The weights will slow down the movement of his legs and he'll run slower, in the same way tension will hamper the movement of your muscles and slow down your clubhead.

Tension will not only decrease clubhead speed, it also will interfere with proper clubhead rotation and forward-swing path, both of which are crucial to the accuracy of your shots.

Try this: Swing the club while keeping your hands, wrists and arms intentionally stiff. You'll find that you won't get much motion. Then, relax your muscles, beginning with your shoulders and upper arms first, then moving down to your elbows, then forearms, then wrists, while still maintaining control with your fingers. That may prove tricky at first. Try to keep the club under control with your hands without allowing the wrists and arms to tighten up. Take another swing and feel the difference between before, when you were stiff, and now, when you're relaxed. You'll

BRUTE FORCE

The majority of golfers use brute force to hit the ball. They tense up when they swing at the ball, cutting the clubhead speed and disrupting the forward-swing path.

see there's a lot more motion when you're relaxed. So, although it may sound like a paradox, you've got to reduce your effort in order to hit the ball farther.

What feels like less effort will actually give you more clubhead speed. Remember: Speed Equals Distance — Motion Creates Speed — Less Tension Creates More Motion.

Often, I find it isn't hard to convince someone who's ball-bound of that idea. In fact, they understand it easily and are eager to try to swing without tension, but when they step up to the ball, they react as always and end up tightening up somewhere before impact. These are almost always the people who are capable of making fairly fluid practice swings, but can't bring themselves to use that same swing over the ball. That's why I call it being "ball-bound" — because the presence of the ball binds their swing with tension.

A LITTLE TENSION EQUALS A LOT OF DAMAGE

It's pretty obvious to most people that a lot of tension is going to restrict the motion of the swing, but the fact is it only takes a little tension to have a large adverse effect. No matter how loose you are at address and at the start of the forward swing, all fluid motion will be lost if even the smallest surge of tension occurs before impact. At worst, besides cutting clubhead speed, tension will also interfere with proper clubhead rotation and good forward-swing path, both of which will hurt your accuracy. For you to hit your best shots, the clubhead must flow smoothly, nonstop from the start of the forward swing through to the top of the finish without even the slightest hesitation, interruption, surge, jerk or pull.

The habit of being ball-bound is difficult to break, because you've already conditioned yourself to swing that way when you are hitting a shot. It's easy to make a relaxed practice swing when you know there's nothing to interfere with the motion of the clubhead. Because you've been trained by so many past swings to tense up when you see a ball behind the clubface at address, like any bad habit, it takes time to change. Simply telling your body not to do something by using a verbal command is no guarantee. You have to train your muscles to remain relaxed when you swing through the ball.

Remember "Señor Loopy"? He was the worst case of being ball-bound I've ever seen. His practice swing was quite relaxed, but his "ball swing" was extremely tight, loopy and jerky. The difference between his practice swing and real swing was easily the most drastic I'd ever witnessed. While working with him, I had no problem getting him to make his practice swing even looser than it was, but whenever he stepped up to the ball he would revert back to his usual slashing action. Finally, I asked him to make a practice swing, which he performed effortlessly and with good form. Then, I stood in front of him and held a ball up to the level of his eyes and asked him to watch the ball while he made another practice swing. He fixed his gaze on the ball I was holding and swung, but the swing he made was nothing like his usual practice swing — it was the same tense, loopy lurch he normally made whenever he swung at a ball. For him, the mere sight of a ball, whether he was trying to hit it or not, was enough to incite the ball-bound reaction! You might want to try this test yourself: Have a friend hold a ball up at about eye-level, then focus on it when you make a practice swing and see if it produces tension. You may be surprised to find out.

BREAKING THE BALL-BIND

Unless you break the habit of being ball-bound, the rest of this book will be no use to you. My system will only work if you rid your swing of this type of tension, and if you don't do that, then you can't make progress. So it's imperative you pay attention here and break the ball-bind if you are afflicted with it.

The reason people become ball-bound is that they focus too much on the moment of impact, trying to control the clubface squareness to the ball. To cure the ball-bind, you must shift your focus away from the ball/impact and onto something else. The best thing to shift your focus toward is the motion of the clubhead and what it feels like as it swings forward into the finish. Make sure you always give yourself easy lies sitting up on good grass or a tee. Then work gradually to tighter lies.

When it comes to sensing the clubhead, most people are aware of it to some degree, but they aren't feeling it nearly as much as they need to in order to make a free swing. That's because tension cuts down on your sense of feel — the tighter your wrists, forearms and shoulders are, the less you can sense the clubhead. The more feedback you start getting from the clubhead, the less tension you'll have in your swing. If you work on shifting your focus to the motion of the clubhead and away from the ball or body movements, you'll eventually stop tensing up during the swing.

Another thing that will help when trying to break the ball-bind is to move your visual focus away from where it usually is onto something else. Again, because most golfers pay the most attention to what they see rather than what they feel, they can't help but associate tension with the sight of the ball. A radical way to change your visual focus is to shift it completely away from the ball by closing your eyes. That will heighten your other senses toward feeling the clubhead while completely eliminating any visual images you might associate with being ball-bound.

Besides only making practice swings, I recommend trying to hit some practice balls with your eyes closed. Be careful with this — find a spot on the range where you won't be able to hit anyone if you spray one badly. I'd recommend limiting yourself to half-length half-speed swings with an easy club like a seven or eight iron, because the point of this drill isn't to hit great shots but to gain familiarity with focusing on the clubhead motion without tension; so don't worry about what the shots look like, how far they go, or even if you make contact at all.

You'll find that because you don't know exactly where the ball is, you won't know precisely when to flinch in response to impact. Thus, you'll start to get to know what it feels like to make contact with the ball without tension, and eventually, you'll come to trust that feeling, and that is a huge step toward making a better swing and hitting longer, straighter shots.

One other approach I like to prescribe to people who are particularly fixated on the image of the ball is to have them make a lot of practice swings while focusing on a ball that lies on the ground just out of reach of the clubhead. By taking practice swings over and over while watching a ball, you will come to associate the sight of the ball with a free swing, so that eventually you'll be able to address a ball and associate the sight of it with the feeling of freedom, not tightness.

OTHER CAUSES OF TENSION

After you break the ball-bind, don't think that you are through with tension — it can also arise randomly from sources other than the ball. Here are the major ones you are likely to run into and some ways to deal with them.

COMPETITION

How often do you feel your swing tighten up when you're competing? Tension is very often brought on by competition, when there is some kind of reward that can be earned by playing well. Usually that reward is winning, whether it's a match or a tournament, and the satisfaction that goes with winning. Competition affects everyone differently, depending on the individual. To some, winning isn't everything, so they don't feel as much pressure. To others, winning is the only thing, so they are more subject to competitive pressure. Tension can be compounded when you not only want to win, but you're also afraid of losing. No one likes to lose, but some like it less than others.

Of course, the level of competition (your desire to play well) also determines how much tension is generated. You may not feel as much tension when competing with your friends in a friendly two-dollar Nassau as you would if you were playing in your club championship.

You don't necessarily have to be playing in an organized competitive situation to feel competitive pressure. When playing with someone you want to impress or teeing off in front of a large group of people on the first hole, you feel pressure to perform well because of the desire to make a good showing for those people. Even after I'd been playing for a while I felt that same kind of nervousness when I took my first lesson from Bob Toski. I wanted to do well in front of him and didn't want to embarrass myself.

Another common type of competition is when you are competing against yourself, which is really the only true competition. We all have been in the position where we are playing extremely well and have a chance to shoot our lowest-ever score. As soon as you realize this, your first instinct is to try to control or guide the club to the ball. This stems from the fear you won't be able to continue playing well and that you may somehow blow everything by having a bad hole.

Whenever your playing circumstances create tension, it's because you are focusing too much on the circumstances rather than on the feeling of the swing needed to execute a given shot. When you hear a pro being interviewed after hitting a miraculous shot under pressure, a commonly used phrase is "I just tried to make a good swing." However, after a bad shot the same pro might say, "I hit poorly because I got to thinking a little too much about that water. . . ." Instead of allowing yourself to dwell on the circumstances, whatever they may be, the best thing to focus on is the smooth forward motion of the clubhead — where it should always be anyway. Focusing on clubhead motion is also particularly helpful because it's a long, continuous action that will keep your mind fully occupied throughout the swing, and by focusing on a smooth motion you'll be more likely to make it happen. The shot will take care of itself, pressure or no pressure.

CONDITIONS

Specific playing conditions are one of the chief sources of random tension. Conditions can range from the kind of lie you have on a particular shot to the weather that day, to the difficulty of the shot you're facing. The tension that results from facing a demanding situation will affect your performance, which is why we often end up failing miserably under these circumstances. When was the last time you tried to drive the ball down a narrow fairway between the trees, but ended up tightening up and pushing or pulling the shot smack into them? Or tried to hit the ball a little harder than usual into a headwind or carry the water and ended up mishitting the shot badly? Or fluffed a chip from a tricky greenside lie? Usually, it's the tension brought on by the condition, rather than the condition itself, that causes the failure.

Again, as when under competitive pressure, your best bet when playing conditions are more difficult is to forget about the conditions and any verbal commands they may inspire — "do this, do that" — and instead shift your focus onto the motion of the clubhead.

VERBAL COMMANDS

When you let your analytical side get too active and start telling yourself to do something specific, like "swing slow" or "stay down on the ball," you're thinking instead of feeling. Usually the more adamant you become — "darn it, I'll stay down to the ball if it kills me!" — the more tension you'll cause.

DISTANCE

Typically, when a person wants to get a little more distance than usual from a particular club — usually the driver — the instinct is to tighten up and use Brute Force. As mentioned earlier, however, BF may work well for moving a heavy object slowly, but when it comes to swinging a light clubhead quickly, BF is greatly detrimental. Most people can swing relaxed and smooth when they swing slowly but have difficulty doing so when the swing speed is increased. As you increase your speed, swing looser and smoother.

HABIT

Some people are tight and manipulative because they were tense the first time they ever swung a club, and they've never known a different feeling. For them, tension is a habit. Such tension can occur not only in the hands, wrists, arms and shoulders, but also in the chest and back, where tightness will restrict your arms from swinging the way they're supposed to.

Habitual tension is more common than you think, because many people approach learning something new with apprehension. Instead of relaxing, they get tense. (You see this a lot among women when their husbands are trying to teach them to play!) As I mentioned earlier, the first time I ever got on skis I was stiff as a board, but fortunately I had an instructor who told me right off the bat that I had to loosen up. In golf, however, most people start out by fooling around on their own, and many have never taken a lesson at all. So if you suffer from excessive tension, it could be that it comes from having been tight since Day One. You just don't know any better. If that's the case, you can learn to get rid of that tension. You won't believe how much better your shots will be when you do.

7

FINDING YOUR FUNDAMENTALS

How do I address the ball? I say, "Hello there ball. Are you going to go in the hole or not?"

Flip Wilson
The Flip Wilson Show (1972)

Before you can start swinging and trying to find the right motion, you need to know the fundamentals — how to hold the club, how to stand up to the ball, etc.

Every book on golf instruction stresses the fundamentals and their importance, so I don't want to rehash a lot of information you might already understand, but I do want to express my thoughts.

Although there is no perfect swing, there are certain fundamentals you must adhere to to establish a good level of success and consistency. I'm not overly concerned about being exact about fundamentals, but I do believe you need to have the discipline to develop good ones and keep them from fluctuating. In my teaching I've noticed most amateurs have a problem with at least one fundamental. And that eventually gets in the way of their ability to reach their potential.

When I think of what I consider to be the fundamentals — grip, posture, stance, ball position and alignment — I don't imagine certain ideals carved in stone, but instead believe each has certain boundaries. In between those boundaries are a variety of acceptable positions. For example, I don't believe that there's one specific grip position that's absolutely correct. Rather, you can lean toward a strong or weak position if you prefer, but again, with certain parameters.

That's not an unpopular view among instructors, most of whom will agree it's okay to vary grip positions within reason.

I believe you have some leeway with regard to almost all the fundamentals. In other words, there is a gray area of correctness you must explore.

Let's begin the exploration.

GRIP

I don't recommend a specific type of grip to my students. Whether you prefer the interlocking, overlapping or ten-finger doesn't matter. Nor do I think it matters exactly how your fingers are placed on the club. What does matter is that your palms face each other and that you allow your fingers to curl naturally around the grip.

Your fingers should allow you to maintain control of the club without the need to exert a lot of pressure. A "tight squeeze" equals unwanted tension in the hands, wrists and forearms. Make sure your fingers lie snug against each other, with no gaps between.

There are two aspects of your grip you'll have to spend some time trapping. The first is grip pressure. You may have read or heard before that it's best to use a relaxed grip pressure. However, your fingers must have a firm enough hold on the handle to maintain control of the club while your wrists, forearms and elbows remain relaxed.

Working with a scale of one to five, with one being extremely light and five being extremely tight, trap the degree of pressure that gives you a secure feeling while at the same time allowing freedom of motion. Pay strict attention to this, because finding the proper finger control with relaxed wrist, forearms and arms is crucial to good clubhead speed and rotation. When trying to determine correct pressure, first make sure the club is secure in your fingers, then tighten the muscles in your wrists and forearms. Next, slowly relax the wrist/forearm muscles until you can sense the weight of the clubhead moving smoothly when you swing it. When you have achieved that feeling, you will have found the proper combination of finger control and freedom in your wrists and forearms that will allow you to swing the club with good speed and proper rotation.

The second aspect of the grip you'll need to trap is grip position. Use the direction the Vs (formed by the thumb and index finger of each hand) point to determine your position. The boundaries they should point between are your nose and just outside your right shoulder. Any grip position between those boundaries is okay, but don't stray outside of them or you'll find it very difficult to return the clubface squarely to the ball without manipulating.

I also recommend to beginners who are learning the grip that when placing their hands on the club they hold the club up, so the shaft points

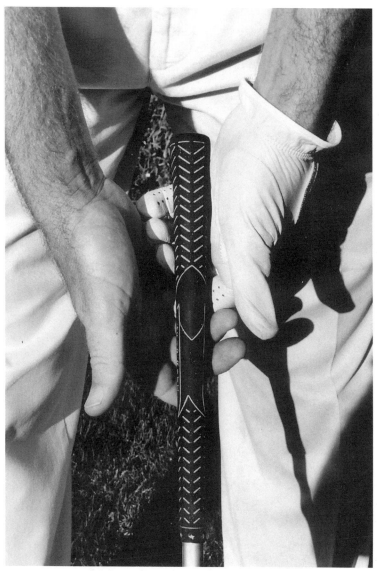

To assume a good grip, first open your palms and lay the club across the crooks of your fingers.

to the sky. Otherwise, when taking your grip while the clubhead rests on the ground, there's a tendency to reach over the top while taking hold with the right hand, causing the shoulders to open and point to the left.

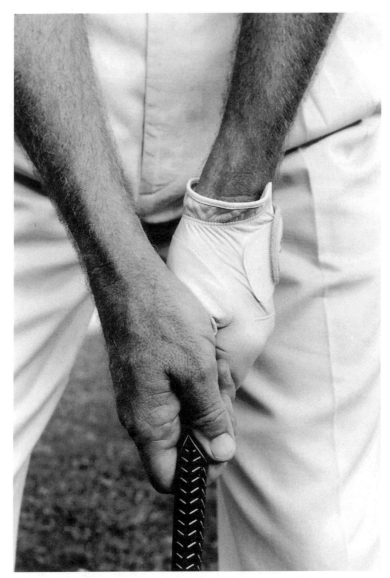

Curl your hands around the club so that your palms are parallel and your fingers have a snug hold with no gaps between them.

Be careful not to exert too much pressure with the fingers. Use light finger control, just enough so the club is not loose in your hands.

The V's formed by the thumb and index fingers of each hand should point somewhere within the "safety zone" formed between your right eye and right shoulder.

Beginners should assume their grip with the club pointing up in the air, since taking hold while the clubhead rests on the ground often results in an open shoulder alignment.

POSTURE

The posture you assume must allow your arms to move freely and your feet, ankles and knees to be active during the swing while at the same time enabling you to maintain your balance between the balls and heels (front and back) of your feet. My own formula for finding proper posture is to first stand up straight, feet spread about shoulder width. Then bend forward slowly at the crease below your hip bones, keeping your back straight and allowing your arms to hang relaxed. Stop bending as soon as you feel your weight move slightly forward, toward your toes. Next, flex slowly at your knees until you feel your weight move back until it is evenly distributed between the balls and heels.

Posture has a great deal to do with dictating proper swing plane. Proper swing plane will be easier to accomplish as long as you have good posture, which allows the sole of the club to lie flat on the ground at address. From there, swing plane will take care of itself if you make sure your hands are somewhere between the boundaries of your right ear and right shoulder at the top of your backswing, and between the top of your left shoulder and left ear at the finish.

To assume proper posture in three steps, first take a club and stand normally.

Second, bend slowly at the crease below your hips so your weight moves forward onto the balls of your feet, while at the same time keeping your back straight and allowing your arms to hang down relaxed.

Third, flex your knees slowly until your weight has moved back to where it is evenly distributed between the balls and heels of your feet.

STANCE

Stance is nothing more than how you position your feet, and again, there is a lot of leeway. The width of your stance, or how far apart your feet are, should depend on comfort and balance. To find the correct width, start out by assuming a very narrow stance, with your feet close together. When you swing you'll get an unstable feeling, and may even lose your balance. Gradually spread your feet apart until you obtain a sense of complete control and balance even when you make a full, fast swing. Take care, however, that your feet aren't so far apart that the stance restricts your weight shift and the movement of your lower body. Generally, the width of your stance for your driver is somewhere between the width of your shoulders or slightly wider. From there, your stance should naturally grow narrower to accommodate shorter-shafted clubs.

As far as individual foot position goes, most people like to point each one outward a little, which is fine as long as the angle doesn't go beyond a reasonable amount. You also have the option of squaring your right foot, which many golfers do to keep from overswinging or losing balance at the top.

Your feet should be spread about shoulder width, varying to slightly wider with long-shafted clubs and slightly narrower with short-shafted clubs. Both feet should be angled outward slightly, though some players may prefer to square the right foot.

BALL POSITION

Where you position the ball is simple because it should be automatically determined by where your left arm hangs. All you need to do is, without a club, assume proper posture and stance and allow your left arm to hang. Then, place the club in your left hand. This will determine where the clubhead rests on the ground, and the ball should be positioned just opposite the face. That is your ideal ball position, both in terms of where it is located in your stance and how far away you should stand from it.

The reason the ball should not be automatically positioned opposite the left heel (as is often recommended) is because doing that may require you to contort your set-up slightly in order to accommodate where the ball is located, and may also force you to manipulate the club in an attempt to shift the bottom of your swing arc in order to strike the ball solidly. Instead, let the position of the ball accommodate your set-up. That way, it will automatically be located in or at the bottom of your arc.

Having said all that, typical ball position should range somewhere between your left heel and an inch or two inside it, if the rest of your set-up is correct. If the ball lies outside these boundaries, it's an indication your stance may be too wide or too narrow. The one exception to this is the driver, where some players prefer to play the ball a little forward of the left heel, opposite the instep.

Note: Players who are ball-bound normally stand a little closer to the ball than they should. That's because when they tense up on the downswing, their arms contract inward a little, so in order to "find" the ball with the center of the clubface, they have to crowd it slightly. Once the ball-bind is broken and you are relaxed on the forward swing, your arms will extend more through impact. You'll then probably have to adjust to a new ball position that's a little farther away from your body in order to find the ball with the clubface.

Where your left arm hangs should dictate ball position. Assume your address without a club, then insert a club in your left hand.

The ball should be positioned squarely opposite where the clubhead rests.

How far you stand from the ball should also be determined by where the clubhead rests on the ground when you grip with your left hand.

ALIGNMENT

Alignment has to do with how and where your body and the clubface are aimed. Of all the fundamentals, alignment is the most important because it has the most to do with your accuracy, and since golf is a target-oriented sport, accuracy is crucial — the closer you hit the ball to the target with every stroke, the fewer overall strokes you'll end up taking. Most amateurs, however, suffer from some degree of poor alignment. Pros, on the other hand, are much better at aiming, which is one of the reasons they drive the ball more accurately, hit it closer to the hole more often and get more distance.

Generally, the better you are aimed at the target, the closer to it you'll hit the ball. I say "generally" because it isn't always necessary that you aim directly at the target. In golf, it is possible to aim left or right and then manipulate the forward-swing path and clubhead release in order to direct the ball toward the target. Usually, both the poor alignment and the manipulation are unconscious. If you ask the player who aims poorly where he's aimed, he'll usually tell you "at the target," because that's where he thinks he's aimed. When this kind of misalignment and manipulation occur, it's usually a case of the player aiming to the right of the target, then manipulating the club in order to re-route the clubhead path back across the line toward the target.

You'll swing more efficiently and be more accurate if you align yourself *parallel-left* of the target line. This applies to right-handed players, and means that your body-lines are on the left side of the target line and parallel to it. Left-handed players should be parallel-right. Aligning yourself parallel-left is best, because then you can swing freely without having to manipulate the club to hit the ball toward the target, allowing you to create maximum speed with minimum effort. Also, if the shot isn't completely accurate, the ball still shouldn't end up too far from your target.

The key areas you need to pay attention to in terms of aligning your body correctly are your feet, hips, shoulders and eyes. If their lines are parallel to the target line or very close to being parallel, your alignment is acceptable. But if they are pointing well to the right or left of the target line, then your alignment needs to be adjusted back to parallel.

Although proper alignment is a simple idea to understand, being able to assume it and aim correctly is completely different. Very few amateurs have trained themselves to consistently align themselves correctly. In-

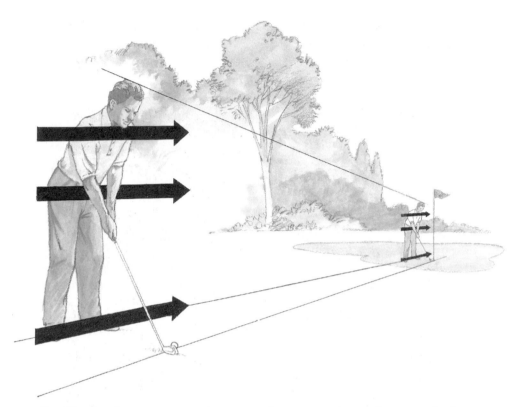

You'll enjoy far greater consistency and accuracy if you align your body lines parallel-left of the target line (feet, hips, shoulders and eyes).

stead, as mentioned before, most make the mistake of aiming their bodies to the right of the target line, then compensate for that with an outside-in forward-swing direction. Besides resulting in poor accuracy, this also causes a tremendous loss in clubhead speed. It's similar to when a power hitter in baseball swings at an inside pitch: Instead of his arms being able to swing freely, they will be jammed in close to his body, with less freedom to move. The result is a loss of motion and, thus, power. I suffered from this problem for a long time without realizing it.

I understood the need to aim parallel-left because I had read about the importance of it in books and magazines and witnessed it in good players I had played against in tournaments and seen on television. But although I *thought* I was aligning my body correctly, parallel-left of the target line, it took Bob Toski to point out I was aiming thirty yards to the right. I was stunned. Even though I knew I should aim parallel-left, the problem was that I hadn't learned how to do it. There is a big difference between understanding what to do and doing it.

Occasional use of a pointer club while practicing will help you enforce good alignment and swing habits by training your eyes to aim your body parallel left of target.

You'll have an easier time aiming if you picture a powerful image for a target line, which is why I like to imagine a trench a foot wide running from the ball to my target.

It's relatively easy to look down and check to see whether your body lines are square with each other, whether your feet, hips or shoulders are out of position. A good procedure is to first square your shoulders up by addressing a ball. Then, keeping your eyes focused on the ball, note the

To increase the chances of setting up parallel left, you must look continuously between the target, the target line, and the ball as you align yourself.

position of your shoulders with your peripheral vision. If you can see both shoulders evenly, then they are square with the line of your eyes. If you can see one shoulder more than the other, then they are not square. You should adjust them until you can see both evenly. Once your shoulders and eyes are square with each other, use them as a reference point to square up the rest of your body — hips, knees and feet — with a visual check.

What's more difficult is determining whether your body is aligned parallel with the target line or not. To check, pick out a target and set up so that you feel you are aiming parallel-left of the target line. Then lay the club you're holding on the ground, just outside your toes and parallel to them. Step away, behind the ball, into a position where you can see exactly where the clubshaft is pointing in relation to the target. If you were aligned correctly, the shaft will be parallel-left to the target line. If you're aimed to the left, the shaft will point left of the target, but not parallel. If you were aligned to the right, the shaft will point right. To get into the habit of assuming proper alignment, adjust the club on the ground so it is parallel to the target line, then set yourself up squarely with it. It will help to continue practicing with a "pointer club" in order to train your eyes to recognize when you are aligned correctly.

Even if your alignment is generally sound, it's a good idea to check it periodically with a pointer club, since alignment has a tendency to slide out of kilter from time to time. If you've ever been to a professional tournament and strolled by the driving range you've probably seen at least one pro employing a pointer club, which is another reason why pros exhibit consistently better alignment and are better at aiming than amateurs — they understand how important it is and work harder at maintaining this important fundamental.

Although a pointer club is a big help during practice, you obviously aren't allowed to use one while you play, so you must train yourself to assume proper alignment without it. That's where you have to use your imagination to give yourself a vivid picture of the target line as an aid. The mistake most people make when they try to do this, in my opinion, is that they don't form a strong enough mental image. They picture a thin, flimsy line running from the ball to the target. Instead, I like to get behind the ball and imagine a long trench, a foot wide. Once you've got something that powerful etched in your mind you'll be ready to address the ball. But it's still crucial that you continually shift your gaze between the target, the target line and the clubface as you turn your body and assume your address position. This will keep the image of the target line strong in your mind so you can be assured of aligning both your body and the clubface squarely to it. Be *extremely* careful when you set the clubhead behind the ball and step into your address position that you don't accidentally set up close to the target line — a chronic mistake.

Good alignment takes discipline. You have to follow the procedure carefully before *every* shot if you want to have the best chance of aiming accurately and not allowing bad habits to form.

8

BUILDING A FREE SWING:
FEEL, FORM AND FINESSE

Take it easily and lazily because the golf ball isn't going to run away while you're swinging.

Sam Snead
How to Play Golf (1946)

The three elements that, combined, make up the technical stages of learning the swing are feel, form and finesse. Each must be learned and developed, one at a time and in order; then all three will blend together to form a sound swing. You will not fulfill your potential as a player unless you cultivate all three.

Feel is the combined freedom and smoothness of the technical movement that gives the swing rhythm, grace and beauty. Tension destroys feel.

Form is the correct combination of body and club motion that gives proper shape to the swing. Form must be learned at a slow pace, similar to when you learned to write your name. Basic form will naturally accompany feel and rhythm; then form can be refined and adjusted, and the speed can be increased.

Finesse is the ability to precisely control the speed and movement of the clubhead while maintaining freedom of motion, allowing you to hit a variety of exacting shots. This is the element that good players focus on when playing. Tension also destroys finesse.

All three of these elements, when put together, equal long, straight, controlled golf shots. Again, each element should be honed in order. Imagine you wanted to program a robot to swing a club. First, you'd program it to make a swinging motion — feel. Then you would program the proper technical movement — form. Finally, you'd program in the precise speed and direction of the clubhead — finesse. You should "program" yourself in the same order.

THE RELATIONSHIP BETWEEN FEEL AND FORM

In golf, motion equals distance. I would much rather see a person focus on maintaining constant freedom of motion than working on a picture-perfect swing with specific technical positions. There's a direct relationship between feel and form. Given good fundamentals, the better your sense of feel for the rhythm and motion of the clubhead, the better your form will be.

Most golfers obsess on "swing mechanics." They worry too much about where their right elbow is pointing at the top or whether they've turned their hips a full 45 degrees. I have certain guidelines I like my students to follow in regard to form, but I've always felt becoming over-specific with technique is a waste of time. If your fundamentals are sound and your feel for rhythm is good, then form will almost take care of itself.

Start by swinging the club slowly and smoothly through the proper technical areas. As you do this you will be blending motion with good positions. This creates a proper sequence of movements and will give you the feeling of good rhythm. And good rhythm is the key to the working relationship of feel and form. Tension will ruin this relationship because it reduces motion and feel. Both are needed to develop and maintain good rhythm.

A great way to help develop good form through motion is to swing very slowly while watching yourself in a mirror or some other reflective surface. When I say watching yourself, I mean your reflection, as opposed to filming yourself on a video camera and watching the tape. By watching yourself as you perform, like a dancer in a mirror, you can see and feel what your body and club are doing and monitor yourself at the same time. Check yourself from directly in front (face-on), from the left (as if looking from the target toward yourself) and from the right (as if looking from behind, straight down the target line). If you detect an error, you can change it immediately. You can see and feel the change at the same time.

Developing good feel allows you to forget about the mechanical details of the golf swing, and learn how to swing so the clubface returns as squarely as possible to the ball while traveling on a relatively straight path toward the target at a reasonable speed. This requires a combination of three things: clubhead release, forward-swing path and clubhead speed.

Watching your reflection while you swing is a good way to monitor the six key checkpoints (see Chapter 10).

You won't get all three perfect with every swing, but the closer you come each time, the more consistently sound your shots will be. When you swing with feel, the motion is smooth and free as the clubhead builds speed and rotates gradually. Even if the clubface alignment and forward-swing path aren't perfect at impact and clubhead speed isn't at its maximum, you'll still produce acceptable shots. I like to call it the "gravity swing" because it feels so effortless that it seems that the only force bringing the clubhead downward is gravity.

However, if you don't have good feel, you'll most likely experience tension and manipulation. Lack of smoothness and rhythm leads to inconsistent forward-swing path and abrupt clubhead rotation, so there's a greater chance that the face will be very open or very closed at impact, resulting in wild shots.

If specific technical details were imperative, there would be one perfect swing all the great golfers duplicated, but there isn't. Take a look at the swings of Jack Nicklaus, Lee Trevino and Arnold Palmer and you'll note many differences. Your form *should* vary a little from other players' swings because you are different from everyone else. You will swing with your own individual style.

When you first learned to write, you were trained to shape the letters as technically perfect as possible, copying all the loops and lines according to what was considered ideal. Eventually you began to give your signature its own personal look.

I don't think that people should shy away from being free and creative with their swing. I prefer that you make long, loose, free-motion swings, much the way young children go outside the lines when coloring with crayons. In the beginning that makes learning more fun. Later, you can fine-tune your swing adjustments to stay within the guidelines, while maintaining the freedom of movement that makes it fun.

The game's greats color their swings differently.

Jack Nicklaus swings back on a very upright plane; Raymond Floyd makes a quirky move to the inside on his takeaway; Lee Trevino and Fred Couples drop the club onto a drastically lower plane on the downswing; Curtis Strange moves his head well off the ball on his backswing. All of these players have had a great deal of success despite the fact they aren't textbook perfect.

If you're overly concerned with adhering to the structure of what a good swing should look like, you'll rob yourself of the freedom and creativity that allow you to relax and make a free-flowing, rhythmic swing.

The bottom line: It doesn't matter precisely what your swing looks like as long as you are hitting the ball solidly and accurately with good clubhead speed. Good players are more concerned about what their shots look like than with how perfect their swings look.

9

DEVELOPING FEEL:
FINDING FREEDOM OF MOTION

We are getting too mechanical about the golf swing. Golf was never meant to be an exact science—it's an art form. Einstein was a great scientist but a lousy golfer.

Bob Toski
Golf Digest (1981)

In this chapter we'll look at the specifics of *feel*, how to trade tension for freedom and how to get in touch with the feeling of the clubhead, which is your key to making a smooth, relaxed swing. When you've learned all that, only then can you begin shaping the *form* of your swing.

When applying the principles and exercises put forth in this chapter, I'd like to recommend against hitting golf balls. I've found my students make a lot more progress when they swing without a ball in front of them. There are two reasons for this.

First, you'll be able to break the habit of being ball-bound faster if you work only on swinging. Since one of your goals is to stop focusing on the ball and start focusing on the clubhead, it's better to eliminate the ball from the equation. Second, if you hit balls at this stage, you may become too wrapped up in the results. The fact is, it doesn't matter where the ball goes at this point. Your object isn't to hit good shots yet, but to free up your swing. For now, simply try to bump the ground lightly as you swing. This will lay the groundwork for solid club-to-ball contact when the time comes.

BRUTE FORCE VS. CENTRIFUGAL FORCE

To generate maximum clubhead speed on a correct, unerring forward-swing path, you have to make use of centrifugal force. To do that, allow the clubhead to swing on its natural course rather than trying to guide it, manipulate it or muscle it.

Picture this: You are playing a match against a big, strong opponent. You both tee off, but his drive ends up next to a tree that restricts his

99

backswing. Although he has only 150 yards to the green and he is physically strong, he cannot create the clubhead speed necessary to hit the ball that far. He will most likely make a jerky, awkward swing, using brute force alone, which will not create enough swing speed to advance the ball to the green. You, on the other hand, have no such restriction. Because you can make a full swing, you can build the clubhead speed needed to get your ball to the green. Although you don't have your opponent's strength, you can still generate more speed by coordinating your motion and making a long, smooth swing. The ability to swing the club freely, making use of centrifugal force, is much more effective than trying to swing using brute force.

The dictionary defines centrifugal as "proceeding or acting in a direction away from a center or axis." What should that feel like? It should feel as if the clubhead is being pulled outward and away from you. And your body should feel as though it's following the clubhead into the finish. (A note of caution: Don't try to create this feeling by consciously shoving or forcing your arms to extend or move away from your body, because that requires tension, and tension destroys motion.)

One of my students, a well-known golf writer named Desmond Tolhurst, put the feeling into words another way. Des came to me suffering from tremendous tension. He was very stiff and rigid from his fingers all the way to his toes. After I'd gotten him to relax his muscles and make a few swings, I asked him to describe how it felt. "It feels as if my arms are spaghetti and that someone is holding onto the other end of the club, trying to gently pull it out of my hands," he answered. That is exactly the feeling you'll experience when you swing freely and create centrifugal force.

There are a few exercises that will allow you to compare the difference between centrifugal force and brute force. One is to take a five iron and hold on to it with only your thumb and index finger. Then, try to take the club back very slowly, not swinging the clubhead but instead inching it back halfway, then inching it forward. You'll find that it takes a lot of effort and that it's not necessarily a pleasant feeling — that's brute force. Next, maintain the same hold, but relax your wrists and arms and swing the clubhead gently back and forth. Now you're experiencing motion and speed, courtesy of centrifugal force.

Another exercise is to tie a weighted object like a yo-yo securely to the end of a three-foot length of string and make gentle half-swings, keeping the string taut. To do that you have to keep the action smooth,

Tight Swing

HIGH
TENSION

LOW
CLUBHEAD
SPEED

Free Swing

LOW
TENSION

HIGH
CLUBHEAD
SPEED

Physical tension directly affects clubhead speed: The more tension you exert, the less speed you'll build, while the less tension you exert, the more speed you'll build.

even and rhythmic, especially at the transition between backswing and forward swing, because the string is so flimsy. It takes a focused, coordinated effort on your part to keep the string straight and not allow it to break down. You should also observe that if centrifugal motion is lost due to manipulation (effort) and the string loses its tautness, you also lose control of the motion and path of the object tied to the other end.

When swinging a golf club you don't get quite the same kind of feedback from the shaft. The shaft is stiff and won't break down when you lose centrifugal force. Therefore, you need to focus on the feeling of the clubhead as it swings.

The final exercise is to practice swinging only your arms without a club. As you swing them, shift your focus from your arms to your elbows, then to your hands and finally to your fingertips. With each shift of focus, the motion should feel faster and more effortless than the one before. Why? Because when you focus on swinging just your arms, you tend to concentrate on your shoulders and upper arms, and that results in tension. But by focusing on swinging your fingertips, you naturally relax in order to build motion in what's at the end of your arms — your fingertips. If you apply that principle when holding a club and focusing on the clubhead, you'll generate more speed.

GAINING TRUST IN CENTRIFUGAL FORCE

Learn to trust the feeling of centrifugal force. I've had many students, after experiencing the feeling for the first time, tell me they're afraid the club is going to fly out of their hands. Their response is to hold on tighter to the club which, of course, inhibits both centrifugal force and the freedom of motion. Be aware also that making use of this force doesn't mean swinging slowly. The motion should be loose and smooth, but not slow or sloppy.

TENSION SWINGS: THE "SPIN," THE "PULL" AND THE "TWIST"

The swings of a player who suffers from tension fall into three basic categories — the "Spin," the "Pull" and the "Twist."

THE SPIN

The Spin is characterized by a violent spin of the hips at the start of the forward swing. The Spin throws the upper body out of position and forces the forward-swing path to the outside and over the top. The result is that the clubhead approaches the ball on an outside-in path. The Spin is more commonly known as "coming over the top," and stems from the popular idea that almost all of the power in the golf swing is generated by the spinning of the left hip on the downswing.

There are two problems with this concept. One is that spinning the hips causes the shoulders to spin outside and around the target line. Although your lower body, especially the feet and knees, should assist in creating some additional clubhead speed, most of the speed and control come from your hands and arms. Only through a coordinated motion of your hands, arms, feet and knees can you build centrifugal force. Allowing any one area to dominate or to be separate from the whole flowing motion, especially the lower body, is damaging. A lot of extra torso movement will get in the way of the free-swinging motion of the arms.

The key to curing the Spin is to forget the hips and instead focus on a very gentle change in weight during the forward swing, starting with your feet. If you move your feet and swing the clubhead, then everything else will follow smoothly in succession — the ankles, then the knees, then the hips; then the arms will drop downward naturally (instead of pulling), dropping the club "into the slot." That allows the clubhead to release freely past the body through impact into the finish, instead of shifting outward into an outside-in forward-swing path.

It helps to watch yourself in a mirror to cure the Spin. With the mirror positioned to your right, watch carefully as you start the downswing. Notice how your upper body, shoulders and the club move immediately to the outside if you spin your left hip. Then notice how, if you start down by shifting your weight gently with your feet and knees, your hips and shoulders stay in the correct position and the club stays inside and on the proper swing plane as you swing downward.

The "spin" is characterized by a violent spinning of the hips at the start of the forward swing, which leads to an outside-in clubhead path.

THE PULL

The Pull occurs when you yank the clubhead down from the top with a tense left arm. Besides ruining centrifugal force, the Pull also destroys proper clubhead rotation and the direction of the forward-swing path, usually resulting in an ugly pull-slice. Instead, your arms should start down gradually and smoothly and swing freely past your body as the clubhead releases.

The Pull is probably the most common of the tension-driven swings. It's primarily caused by the myth that the left side should dominate the swing and do most of the work on the downswing. Instead, think of golf as a two-sided game, with both right and left contributing to the motion. Speed, though, must be generated slowly and smoothly, not in one burst from the top or anywhere else. Remember that when you swung the object tied to the string, you had to make a smooth transition between backswing and downswing and then build speed gradually so that the speed peaked at the bottom of the arc. The same smooth transition must happen with a club. If you jerk the club down from the top and pull violently with your left side, you'll ruin the smooth motion and centrifugal force of the clubhead.

Many players are afflicted by the Pull only when they use longer-shafted clubs, because they equate the need to hit the ball a longer distance with the need to use brute force. As such, they pull the club down hard from the top.

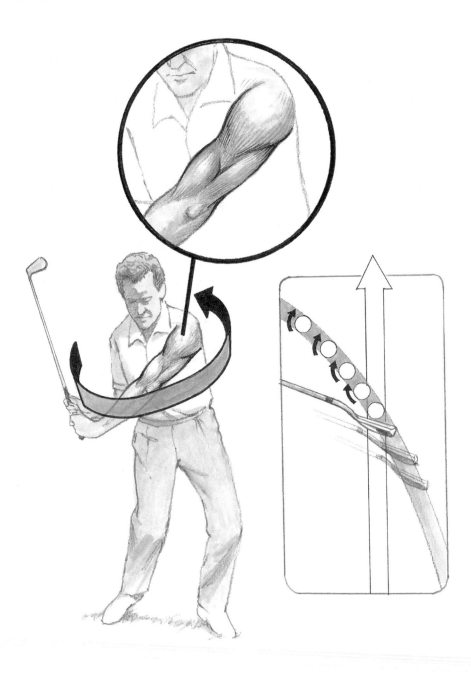

The "pull" happens when you pull the clubhead down sharply from the top with a tense left arm and shoulder, resulting in an outside-in clubhead path and generally an open clubface.

THE TWIST

When you consciously try to release, or square, the clubface on the down-swing by twisting your wrists and forearms, you're suffering from the Twist. If you try to force the club closed, that means you're creating tension — nothing in the swing should be forced. The result of the Twist is a late release, because the tighter your muscles the slower the clubhead will rotate. The result is an open face at impact and a slice. What also may happen is that you sense the clubface is open on the downswing and react by trying to close it quickly, resulting in a closed face at impact, causing either a pull or a smothered hook.

The release should occur without a concerted effort on your part. The clubhead will rotate back to square as it flows through the hitting zone. Those who suffer from the Twist had tension in their forearms and wrists in the first place, preventing the natural release of the clubhead. Because you sensed the face was open through impact, you reacted by trying to force it closed. The motion of the clubhead should rotate your wrists; your wrists shouldn't try to force the clubhead to rotate. Instead of forcing the release, the answer is to relax and simply *allow* the clubhead to swing freely. To get in touch with a good release, it helps to slow every-thing down. Once you've developed a feel for it, you can gradually in-crease clubhead speed without incurring the Twist. Your goal with every club should be to make a smooth, effortless swing — making the most of centrifugal force.

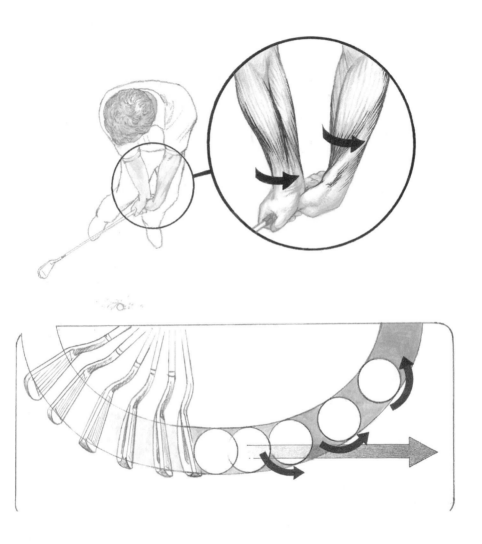

The "twist" occurs when you consciously try to square the clubface by twisting your left and right forearms and wrists, which results in a closed clubface at impact.

GETTING INTO THE PROPER MINDSET

To swing the clubhead smoothly, your mind should be focused on one thing: the motion of the clubhead. I cannot stress that strongly enough. You've probably heard the saying that golf is 90 per cent mental. This is what a lot of that mental energy should be expended on. Focusing on the fluid movement of the clubhead will keep your mind away from distracting thoughts or verbal commands, and instead keep it centered on the feeling of the clubhead and its motion.

LOSING TENSION AND FINDING MOTION IN THREE STEPS

To trade a tight, jerky swing for a relaxed, smooth one, you must exchange tension for a sense of the motion of the clubhead — you can't have both. Your feel for the clubhead should be in terms of its speed, rotation and rhythm. At no point should there be a sudden burst of energy or power — you should instead start the forward swing slowly and build speed gradually so it peaks through the bottom of the arc, then continues into your finish. Any manipulation or sudden tightening of the muscles will interrupt this speed-building process and throw the club off track. Simply swing the clubhead as freely as possible, allowing it to naturally rotate and assume its own forward-swing path — don't do anything to disturb it.

To get in touch with the feeling of free motion, follow these three steps:

Step One: Extend your arm outward and hold on to the end of a five iron lightly between your thumb and forefinger, letting the shaft hang straight down. Swing it gently back-and-forth, back and forth like a pendulum, letting gravity do most of the work as you feel the rhythm of the moving clubhead.

Step Two: Grip the club with your right hand alone and swing it back and forth, letting the club swing down as if it's free-falling. Finish with the club and your hand over your left shoulder. Repeat the motion over and over while trying to duplicate the same rhythm and feeling you experienced in Step One, making sure not to tighten the muscles in your

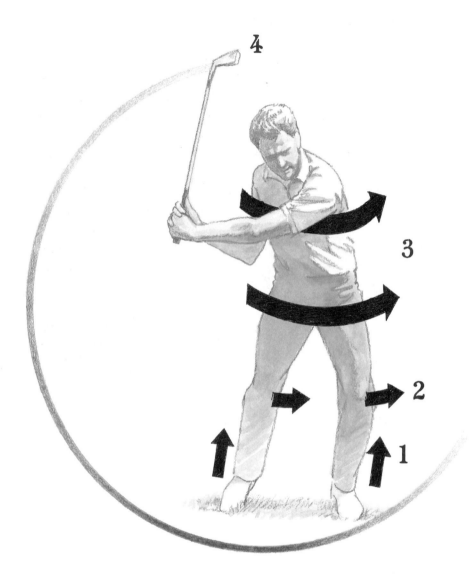

A well-timed and coordinated swing that produces a good clubhead path starts from the ground up: first the feet, followed closely by the knees, and finally the arms and clubhead.

wrist, forearm, elbow or shoulder. Switch to your left hand and do the same.

Step Three: Place both hands on the club and make normal swings, continuing in a back-and-forth, rhythmic motion, letting gravity do almost all of the work while you barely assist. Let the clubhead build speed through the bottom of the arc gradually, like a child on a swing or a string of cars on a roller coaster as it negotiates a dip in the tracks. Forget about verbal directives or body positions and instead expend all of your mental energy on sensing the clubhead movement.

These three steps are designed to heighten your feel for clubhead motion. Once you gain that feeling, you will hopefully never lose familiarity with it. Note that when you start to gain motion in your swing, it's probably going to feel extremely loose and almost sloppy. That's because you're probably accustomed to being tight. If your swing feels too loose, it's a good sign you're doing it correctly. A word of caution, though: Most golfers who are used to swinging with tension usually inadvertently revert back into being too tight, either because they're used to the habit of using brute force or because the club feels as though it's slipping out of their hands. Watch this closely, and if you feel it happening, immediately return to the three steps to regain your feel for the clubhead again.

Step One: Hold a five iron lightly by the end of the grip between your thumb and forefinger.

Swing it gently back and forth like a pendulum.

Step Two: Grip the club with one hand and swing it.

Duplicate the same free, effortless rhythm you felt in Step One.

Step Three: Place both hands lightly on the club and swing.

Again duplicate the same back-and-forth feeling of ease and pace that you experienced in the previous two steps.

COORDINATING YOUR BODY RHYTHM TO THE RHYTHM OF THE CLUBHEAD

To coordinate the rhythm of your body movement with the rhythm of the clubhead, focus on the two contact points in the swing: your hands to the club and your feet to the ground. The feel you get from the clubhead comes through your hands, while the rhythm of the swing is rooted in the relationship of motion between the clubhead and your feet. The way to coordinate the movement of your body with the movement of the clubhead is by focusing on the feelings in your feet and hands. (Remember, focusing on the movement of hips will result in the "Spin" swing.) Let your arms swing and feel the clubhead rotate as your weight moves to your right foot on the backswing, then to your left foot on the forward swing. The rhythm of the clubhead should be similar to a pendulum in that it should start slowly at the beginning, slow down during the change of directions, then move fastest through the bottom of the swing, as if gravity is doing all the work.

USING ALL OF YOUR SENSES TO CREATE MOTION

You shouldn't need a swing-analyzing machine to tell you you're swinging faster and with more freedom; you should be able to sense it. Don't think about specific body positions or motions; instead, just use your sense of *feel*. Again, your hands and arms should feel as though they're moving in a loose and fluid manner, as if they're flying away from your body in the follow-through. Watch your reflection and you should be able to see the difference. Listen and you should be able to hear it in the sound of the clubhead — (whoosh!) — as it accelerates through the bottom of your arc. (One of the things I like about doing this with a driver or three wood is that they make a louder sound when they cut through the air. You can actually hear the clubhead speed.)

SPEED AND SMOOTHNESS MUST GO HAND IN HAND

An extremely important point I'd like to impress upon you as I close this chapter is that whenever you increase the speed of your swing, you must also make a conscious effort to increase its smoothness. The instinct of most people is to tighten up when they try to swing faster. With tightness comes jerkiness, not smoothness.

To marry speed with smoothness, try this exercise. Take a driver and, using a scale of one to five, one being the slowest, make a few swings at level one, slow and smooth. Then increase your speed to levels two, three, four and finally five, taking care that the motion remains even and tension-free each time you turn up the speed a notch, and that the whooshing sound of the clubhead should build gradually until it is at its loudest when the clubhead passes through the bottom of the swing arc — directly in front of you.

SWING THE SAME WAY WITH EVERY CLUB

Use the same free, coordinated swing motion with every club. I often see players swing freely with shorter clubs, but fall back into the trap of using brute force with longer clubs. It's the reason so many amateurs are prone to wild tee shots. With the driver their intention is to crush the ball, but they tense up, make a jerky swing, and wind up hitting a bad shot. When you learn to swing freely and smoothly with every club, driver through wedge, your improvement will be dramatic.

10

SHAPING YOUR SWING FORM

Better to strike a straight blow with a crooked swing than to spend your whole life trying to straighten it out.

Benjamin Franklin's Granddad

Your next step is to add control to motion without losing your new-found freedom. This simply means refining the shape, or *form*, of your swing by eliminating sloppiness and giving more structure to the motion. The goal is to make your swing more consistent and give you more control of your shots. You're like a baseball pitcher who has learned to throw a good fastball, but can't find the plate. His object is to gain control over his motion so he can be more precise with his pitches without losing any speed. You're trying to do the same when you swing the club-head.

THE SIX MAJOR SWING FACTORS

There are six ingredients in a swing.

1. CLUBHEAD ROTATION

The clubhead gradually rotates clockwise during the backswing so the face opens, then rotates counterclockwise on the forward swing so the face returns to square at impact. Clubhead rotation on the forward swing, which is known as the "release," doesn't happen abruptly. The clubface doesn't stay open through the forward swing and then slam shut through impact in a "pull down-release" manner (which is manipulating, not swinging). Instead, the face opens and closes gradually as the clubhead is swung.

This rotation will happen naturally, but only if your arms are relaxed and tension-free. If your swing is smooth and relaxed, you can be confident that the clubhead is rotating correctly.

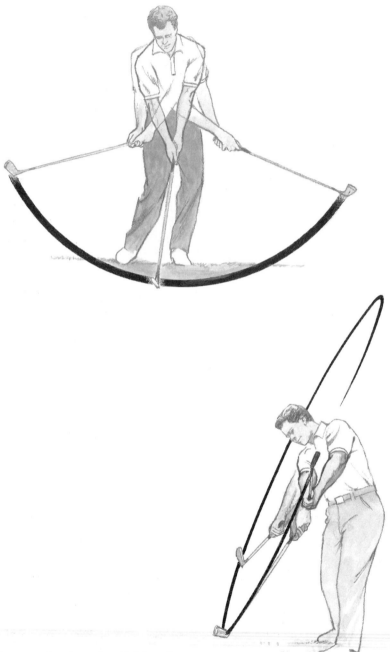

In a good swing, the clubhead rotates open on the backswing, then gradually rotates back to square at impact, and closed in the follow-through. (Notice the clubhead rotation occurs on the swing plan *both* ways). Any snapping of the wrists will rotate the clubhead off the swing angle.

Make a slow swing with a seven iron and watch and feel how this clubhead rotation occurs. When the rotation, or release, is timed correctly, the clubface will be square at impact or very close to it, resulting in a straight or fairly straight shot. (When you make what could be termed a "perfect" swing, with all of the six factors correct, the club will be moving from slightly inside to down the target line, with the clubhead rotating so the face is square at impact. If the clubface rotates very gradually through impact, imparting the slight counterclockwise spin, it creates a draw. If the release is late, the face will be open at impact, imparting clockwise spin on the ball causing a fade or slice.

Therefore, your ability to time the release is directly related to your ability to control the ball, either to hit it straight or to make it curve to the right or left. (More on the specifics of how to intentionally curve shots later in Chapter 12.)

There are certain times when there is a general tendency to release the club too soon: with shorter-shafted clubs, when trying to make a slower swing than usual, and when trying to make a shorter swing to hit the ball a shorter distance than usual, such as a half or three-quarter wedge shot. There are also instances when the tendency will be to release the club too late — with longer-shafted clubs, and when the swing is very fast (which is one of the reasons why a slice usually ensues when the downswing is rushed).

A well-timed release is easiest to execute with shorter to medium-length clubs. However, you should be able to achieve a well-timed release with every club as long as you make a relaxed, smooth swing. If it feels as though gravity is doing the work on the forward swing, then you're almost guaranteed to make a proper release.

Although you can't actually watch the release because the clubhead moves so quickly through the bottom of the swing, you can hear the sound and sense the feeling the club creates as it releases, the *whoosh* of the clubhead as it travels through the bottom of the arc. That whoosh should be centered directly in front of you — through the ball. If the whoosh occurs before the clubhead reaches the bottom of the swing arc, then you're releasing the club too soon. If the whoosh occurs after the clubhead reaches the bottom of the arc, then you're releasing too late. Note: As you increase your swing speed the whoosh tends to occur later in the forward swing — after impact.

If your shots are going to the right, you'll need to focus on releasing

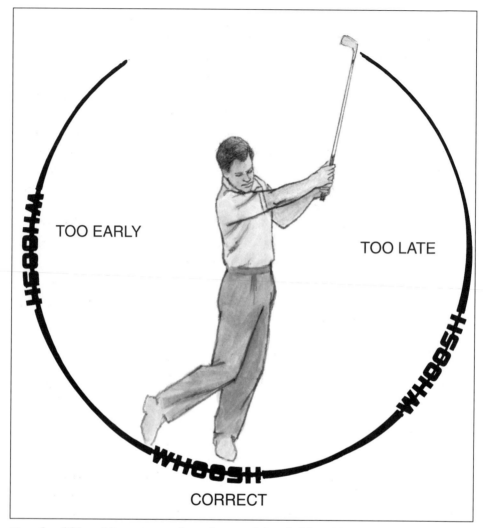

TOO EARLY

TOO LATE

CORRECT

You should be able to sense the release of the clubhead by the sound—whoosh—it makes. If the sound occurs before the clubhead reaches the bottom of the swing arc, then the release is too early. If it occurs after the bottom, then the release is too late. If it occurs directly at the bottom, then the release is timed correctly.

the clubhead sooner in the forward swing. The earlier you release the clubhead, the less the shot will bend right. Conversely, if your shots are going left, it means you're releasing too soon (my problem when I duck-hooked my driver), and the cure is to feel the release happening later in

the forward swing. The more you experiment with releasing the clubhead, the better you'll be able to trap the proper timing of it so the clubface arrives at the ball squarely through impact.

To get more in touch with the rotation of the clubhead, try this exercise: Grip a three iron, close your eyes and point the shaft up, straight out
in front of you. Using feel alone, try to rotate the head slowly so that the
toe is pointing straight up, toward twelve o'clock. Then rotate it to three
o'clock. Then nine o'clock. Then one o'clock. Then eight o'clock. (Open
your eyes each time to check if the position is correct). Your sensitivity to
the clubhead will be increased when you can find each position without
looking.

Another excellent exercise is to try to swing the clubhead back to
square at impact using only one arm. Your natural reaction will probably
be to tighten up with your wrist and/or forearm on the forward swing in
an effort to guide the face back to square. That's manipulation, and it's in-
correct. Instead, relax your shoulders, arms and wrists and allow the clubhead to swing and rotate freely.

2. FORWARD-SWING PATH

Throughout the swing the clubhead travels on a path that is basically a
circle that's on a tilt (as opposed to a Ferris wheel that's vertical). Therefore, to hit the ball toward your target, the clubhead should approach the
ball from slightly inside the target line and make contact when it is moving directly toward the target, before it swings back to the inside.

A poor forward-swing path is caused by poor alignment, in which case
there's really nothing wrong with the path, it's just aiming in the wrong direction. Or, tension and jerkiness can disrupt the path, causing the clubhead to waver and move off-track. (When you flinch before impact, the
clubhead will actually be jerked off a straight path and jolted abruptly inside or outside the swing plane.)

To develop the feel for a proper forward-swing path, first align yourself parallel-left of the target line. Hit a shot while swinging on a very exaggerated inside-out path. Next, hit another, this time with an exaggerated outside-in path. Continue alternating between the two, but concentrate on making the path of each swing a little less exaggerated than the
last until you have trapped a path that sends the ball straight toward the
target. Once you've found the right path, go to work on blending it with a

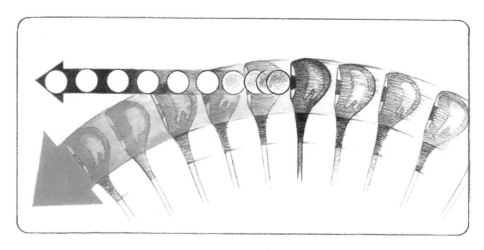

When a proper foward-swing path occurs, the clubhead approaches the ball from slightly inside; make contact when the clubface is square to the target line; then swings back to the inside.

well-timed release. (It's best to do this with the ball teed up while making short, slow swings.)

Poor forward-swing path can also be the result of trying to guide or steer the clubface back squarely to the ball. However, that kind of manipulation throws the club off-path rather than keeping it on-path. There is a great temptation to tighten up and steer your swing when hitting to a narrow fairway or well-guarded green out of fear of missing the mark. This kind of steering usually results in a misguided shot. Instead, a free swing will produce the straight shot you're looking for. It's similar to when you're driving down a straight, empty road. You feel relaxed, your eyes are focused well ahead and your hands are light on the wheel. But suppose you encountered both a narrow bridge ahead and a large truck approaching from the opposite direction. Your first instinct would probably be to try to gain more control by slowing down, tightening your grip on the wheel and focusing on the front of the car. Instead, if you remain relaxed and keep your eyes focused ahead, you'll be able to cruise past the truck and across the bridge with no trouble at all.

3. DOWNSWING ANGLE

Specifically, this is the angle the clubhead travels downward and forward on. Downswing angle will vary from club to club, depending on the length of the shaft. A club with a long shaft, like a wood, will create a larger swing-circle, thus the downswing angle will be fairly shallow. Conversely, a short shaft will result in a smaller, tighter circle, resulting in a steeper downswing angle. That's ideal, because for the best possible distance and trajectory, the clubhead should be moving downward when you make contact with short irons and nearly level to the ground with long irons.

It's important to develop a feel for different angles of approach, from flat and sweeping to steep and downward, and any middle ground in between. (You should also practice hitting on a slightly "upward" angle, so that you are actually trying to scoop the ball up in the air, since this will come in handy if you need to hit a higher than normal wedge shot to get over trouble.) A flat angle should just touch the top of the grass, while a steeper angle should bump the ground more firmly.

When you have gotten reasonably successful at varying your downswing angles, you should start trying to bump the ground in the same place every time — just inside your left heel. Whatever club you use, that is approximately where the bottom of the swing arc should be. Most people who have trouble touching that spot miss by hitting behind it. If so, exaggerate the feeling by trying to touch the clubhead to the ground just ahead of your target spot, and note how it feels. (Generally, it will feel as if your weight is shifting more aggressively to your left side as you swing forward.)

4. SWING LENGTH

When making a full swing, there is no specific backswing length that's right or wrong. Most people can build maximum clubhead speed on the forward swing by taking the club back to three-quarters. Two good boundaries to work between are three-quarters and just slightly past parallel. Normally you'll sacrifice distance or accuracy if you let it go well past parallel, mainly because you're committing some kind of flaw in your form in order to do so, usually either letting your hands and wrists break down or bending your left arm too much.

Downswing angle should vary naturally, depending on the length of the club shaft: steep for short irons, medium for middle irons, and shallow for long irons and woods. With a driver the clubhead must be swung slightly above the ground at the height of the ball.

5. RHYTHM/SWING SPEED

No golfer should swing the clubhead as flat-out fast as he or she possibly can (note I said "fast," not "hard"), for the same reason a pitcher doesn't usually put absolutely everything he has behind his fastball; because by going "all out" you'll sacrifice good rhythm, and will most likely end up with mishit shots.

When I make a full swing, I use about 85 per cent of my speed, which allows me to achieve the proper timing of the sequence of movements that comprise the full swing. In certain situations I might need a little more clubhead speed, such as if I need some extra distance off the tee or I need to hit a wedge harder than usual to get it up high over a tree.

Beware, whenever you try to reach for more speed, you're probably going to sacrifice some body and clubhead control. When I increase to 90 per cent my chances of hitting the ball accurately plummet, so I weigh carefully whether the situation warrants the risk. If you attempt to generate some added clubhead speed, be careful you don't revert to trying to do it through brute force with your torso, shoulders, arms or hands, nor by tightening up. The more body effort you use, the less clubhead speed you produce. To generate extra clubhead speed you need to be looser than usual. The feelings "faster," "looser" and "smoother" should always go together.

Your basic rhythm should smoothly coordinate three key elements: the swinging of the arms, the rotation of the clubhead and the transfer of weight from foot to foot. The clubhead should be traveling slowest at the very start of the backswing (the takeaway) and during the change of directions — the transition between backswing and downswing. It should be traveling fastest through the bottom of the swing. You should work on getting the feel for basic rhythm at slow swing speeds, then gradually increase the pace until you reach what you feel is your optimum speed. If at any time your rhythm is disrupted and your motion gets jerky, slow down the pace until it becomes smooth and then you can begin trying to increase speed again.

When trying to increase speed, pay attention to the sound of the clubhead cutting through the air. A great exercise is to take a driver or three wood and make practice swings, starting slow and gradually increasing the speed, all the time focusing on the "whoosh" the clubhead makes and how much louder it becomes as the speed gets faster. Focus also on

Half swing.

Three-quarter length swing.

Full length swing.

When learning, it's best to start with a short swing and gradually lengthen it to a longer one.

making the sound peak at the very bottom of the swing — directly in front of you — which means that the club is releasing at the right time. (The tendency when trying to add swing speed is to release too late, so that the whoosh occurs later in the swing, past the bottom.) Make sure to keep the motion loose and smooth as you attempt to make it go faster, since any jerkiness will result in a loss of speed and a disruption of swing path and clubhead rotation.

6. SMOOTHNESS

Smoothness is the factor that ties the previous five factors together and allows them to work in harmony. Without smoothness, the first five factors won't blend correctly and you'll make inconsistent contact and get inconsistent results. No one factor is more important than the others. The sum is the whole of its parts. Smoothness, though, is the most abstract of all the swing factors. It's easier to explain the others in words and to demonstrate them with illustrations, but smoothness is more difficult to convey, mostly because it's a *feeling* of all the movements combined. The good news is that it's a feeling that's easy to grasp. I never have any trouble getting my students to pursue the feeling of smoothness when they swing because there's no doubt that a smooth, free swing feels a lot better than a tight, jerky one. Even a complete beginner can identify that a smooth swing motion is more pleasurable than a tense, jerky one. However, you won't swing smoothly simply by telling yourself to do it, because that's thinking, not feeling. You first have to make slow, smooth swings without concern for distance in order to become familiar with what a smooth swing feels like.

Address: Balance evenly distributed in your feet, right elbow relaxed (left elbow for left-handed players).

Halfway back: Clubhead is swung back toward right shoulder, setting the angle between the club and wrists.

Top: Weight to right foot, swing is angled over right shoulder.

**Halfway forward: Weight moved to left foot and knee, arms
and hands swinging club downward.**

Impact: Hands are swinging and releasing clubhead motion through impact.

Finish: Motion of clubhead into the finish moves weight to left foot.

THE SIX KEY CHECKPOINTS OF FORM

Although you can and should be creative with your swing, there are certain guidelines you need to adhere to. It's time to get acquainted with the Six Key Checkpoints of Form.

1. ADDRESS

If you followed the directions in the section on fundamentals, you should be able to assume a good address position. In a good address position your arms should hang as freely as possible and your weight should be distributed evenly between the balls and heels of your feet and evenly between the insides of your right and left foot with all clubs except short irons. When hitting short irons, you may want to shift your weight slightly more toward your left side.

2. HALFWAY BACK

When the club is at the halfway-back point, the clubhead and shaft will be perpendicular to the ground and your hands should be about waist high. The force of the clubhead moving backward, upward and around causes your wrists to hinge so that an angle of about 75 degrees forms between your left forearm and the shaft. Your weight should be moving naturally onto your right foot as your hips and shoulders follow the motion of the club and begin to turn naturally. The clubface should have rotated gradually open, and if someone were watching you from behind, looking straight down the target line, they would be able to see that the shaft is angled just over your right shoulder, parallel to the imaginary line formed between your shoulders and the ball.

3. TOP

At the top of your swing your weight should be almost completely on your right foot and your right knee should still be slightly flexed. Your shoulders and hips should have turned, having followed the free-swinging motion of the clubhead. Your left arm should be relatively straight but free of tightness or stiffness, and your hands should be above your right shoulder. The shaft should be approximately parallel to the target line and the ground. If it is past the point of being parallel to the ground, it should not have been forced into that position. You should maintain finger control on the club while your wrist and forearm muscles stay relaxed. Your left heel should have moved inward slightly in response to the backswing motion.

4. HALFWAY FORWARD

About half of your weight should have been shifted back to your left foot. Your hands and arms should swing the clubhead downward and forward as smoothly and freely as possible, which will allow your shoulders to return to their level set-up position. The strongest thing you feel should be the swinging motion and pulling sensation of the clubhead away from your shoulders and past your body.

5. IMPACT

You cannot consciously get into a specific impact position because everything is moving so quickly at this point in the swing. Therefore, good impact is the result of proper forward-swing motion. However, at impact your weight should be progressively moving more onto your left foot, and the lines of your knees and shoulders should be about parallel to the target line — similar to your address position — as the clubhead swings past your body and rotates gradually through the ball into the finish.

6. FINISH

Your body should be both following and pulled into the finish by the clubhead, which has swung well past your body. All of your weight should be balanced on your left foot as you come up onto the toe of your right foot. The momentum of the follow-through should have pulled your head up so that your back is straight and your arms and hands are relaxed and high over your left shoulder.

Check your reflection to make sure you're approximating these checkpoints. Check also that the clubhead moves in a smooth, unwavering line instead of jumping or waving around. Normally, swinging the club with smoothness and freedom will carry you through each of these positions (except address) without much trouble. By maintaining a smooth motion and periodically reviewing these six checkpoints, you'll be guaranteed to keep such flaws to a minimum.

11

CONTROLLING YOUR LEARNING ENVIRONMENT

Pressure is something every golfer feels at one time or another . . . Sometimes when I putted, I looked like a monkey trying to wrestle a football.

Sam Snead
Golf Digest (1970)

In Chapter 1, I mentioned that playing better golf is based more on how we learn than on how much info we accumulate. This is where we get into that. By now, you should have made strides toward ridding your swing of tension, finding more freedom of motion and improving your form. Now is the time to start hitting practice balls with your new swing, time to start trapping each swing factor — what I call "refining" or "fine-tuning." When refining your swing, I'd strongly advise isolating each of these factors, one at a time. Trying to deal with them all at once is like trying to juggle six objects before you know how to juggle two or three.

In the refining phase, start by combining clubhead rotation and smoothness. Simply getting the hang of these two will make a huge difference in your game. Next, turn your attention to the forward-swing path, followed by the downswing angle. (Some factors may require little or no work. If you are combining smoothness with good form, most of these factors will take care of themselves.)

When you begin, I'd recommend you "control" the learning environment by making things as easy on yourself as you can. Take control by:

1. Using a short-shafted, high-lofted club
2. Teeing the ball up
3. Making a less-than-full swing
4. Swinging at a moderate speed

Controlling your learning environment will make it easier to make solid contact. And that will make it easier to trap each specific swing factor.

How much "control" you need will depend on your position on the trust ladder. With a beginner, I have him take slow half-swings with a nine iron, with the ball teed high on a peg. A low-handicapper, on the other hand, may feel completely comfortable making three-quarter swings with a five iron, off fluffy lies at three-quarter speed. Just remember to make things as easy as you can before you increase the level of difficulty.

The next step is to make things more difficult. Tee the ball progressively lower. Once you acquire a feel for performing each factor, lengthen your swing and increase the speed of your swing gradually. Move up to the next longer club, then to the next. Your ambition should be to reach the point where you can make consistently solid contact while swinging fully, producing a consistent shot pattern (draw, fade or relatively straight) along with consistent divot depth and direction.

Controlling your learning environment is an extremely effective tool for learning and relearning skills. This technique is often met with resistance by some students. Typically the person who is hesitant about following this approach is not a beginner, but rather someone who's been playing golf for a while. The major complaint is "I can't play like this," in reference to the shorter, slower swing they're supposed to start with. If you were teaching a friend how to drive and he couldn't keep the car straight traveling at twenty-five miles per hour, you wouldn't tell him to step on the gas. You'd have him drive at a pace where he could control the car, maybe ten miles per hour. Once he's comfortable he could increase gradually until he reaches the point where he can cruise smoothly at fifty-five. But to get to that level of skill he has to start slow.

The problem with many golfers is that they've been driving crooked at fifty-five miles per hour for a long time, and they dislike the idea of slowing down. Be patient, slow down, control the conditions, and you'll soon be back swinging at normal speed and getting better results. If you can't do it at slow speed, don't speed it up.

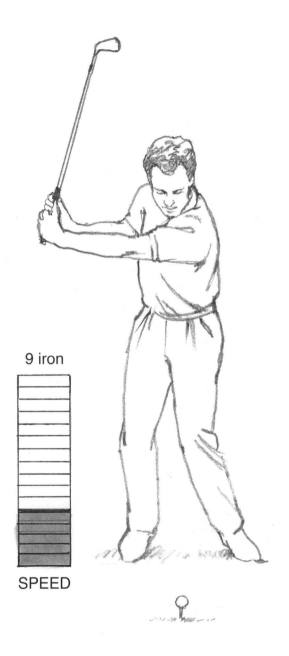

9 iron

SPEED

Exerting maximum control: Ball teed high, short shaft, short swing at slow speed.

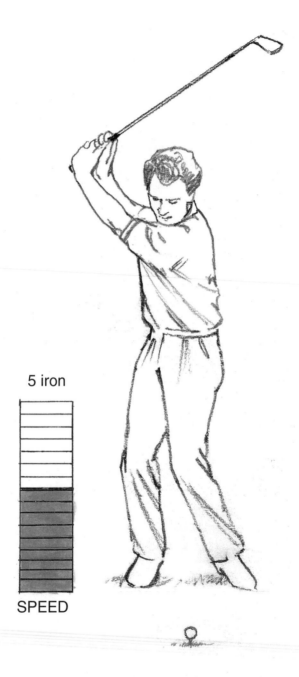

5 iron

SPEED

Exerting minimum control: Ball teed medium-high, medium-length shaft, three-quarter-length swing at moderate speed.

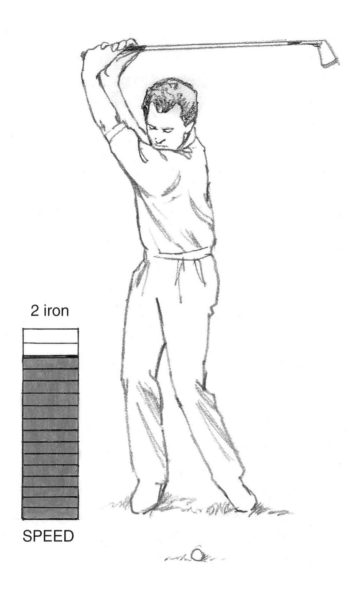

2 iron

SPEED

Exerting no control: Ball on ground, long shaft, full swing at full speed.

FOCUS ON WHAT YOU WANT

When learning, you should always focus on the feelings you want (feelings of smoothness and freedom), and forget about everything you don't want. If you were to ask someone how to get to a certain location and they started telling you how not to get there — "Don't take a right on Lexington Avenue and don't take a left on Sullivan Street" — you would certainly stop them and ask them to tell you where to go, not where not to go. So when learning to swing, focus on the feelings and motions you want. Don't try to fix everything you don't want.

REMEMBER THE GOOD, FORGET THE BAD

When you first start hitting balls, don't be concerned about the results. Remind yourself that learning is a gradual process, that results may come gradually, too. Hitting a golf ball well requires so much precision that you need only be off a little bit to hit a poor shot.

So although you may be well on your way to developing a good swing, your shots may not reflect that right away. The fact is, hitting a poor shot doesn't necessarily mean you made a poor overall swing. One of my students once said to me, "Dean, sometimes I completely miss it—why?" "Because the club is traveling too high above the ground at impact," I responded. She had a fairly sound swing, but wasn't yet acquainted with the feeling of touching the clubhead to the ground properly.

The important thing is that you develop a free-flowing motion first. Most people equate a bad shot with failure and get down on themselves about it, but that won't enhance learning. Dolphin trainers don't yell at, beat or in any other way punish a dolphin when it doesn't perform correctly. The trainer instead will reward it by feeding or petting it when it does the right thing, no matter how long he has to wait. Rather than chewing yourself out when you do poorly, praise yourself when you do well. Focus only on the feelings you want, not those you don't want. For example: Don't try to swing slow when you're over the ball. Focus on swinging the same speed as your rehearsal (practice) swing.

RESUME CONTROL OF YOUR ENVIRONMENT IF TROUBLE STRIKES

Whenever you experience trouble with your swing, you should go back and assume control over the level of your learning environment. That's one of the secrets to solving swing problems quickly. Simplifying and slowing things down makes it easier to detect and correct a problem — and builds awareness. In trouble? Drop down a level on the trust ladder to where you're comfortable, and start working your way back up again.

It's also a good idea to start at a lower level when you're warming up to play. Start at a level where you're completely comfortable when you loosen up so you can build confidence in your swing before you play. Pros do it by starting with half-wedges and working up through the bag, hitting the driver last.

THE IMPORTANCE OF THE PRACTICE SWING

Before you hit any shot, you should make a practice swing. Most golfers make one of three mistakes when they take a practice swing.

One, they make a mindless half-swing, more out of habit than anything else. Players who do this might as well not bother.

Two, although they pay attention to making a smooth practice swing, they then forget the practice swing feeling and instead focus on the ball, causing them to tense up and make a jerky swing.

Three, they make a smooth practice swing, but at a very slow speed; then instinctively try to "give it a little extra" when they get over the ball by pushing, shoving or jerking the club downward.

The purpose of a practice swing is to help you capture the feeling of the kind of swing you want to use on the ball. With that feeling fresh in your mind, repeat it when you hit the shot. I also like to refer to a practice swing as a "rehearsal" swing, because it should be a rehearsal of what's to come. If you don't like the feeling of the first rehearsal swing, keep making them until you're satisfied. Then hit the ball with that swing feeling. The swing you hit the ball with should be an exact copy of your best practice swing in length, speed and smoothness. If you find you're having a hard time getting the hang of that, back down to an easier situation: A shorter, slower swing, or a pitch or chip shot. If, however, you've acquired the knack of making a good practice swing but your shot results aren't acceptable, you're probably suffering from some technical flaw and will need to troubleshoot to fix the problem.

12

STAYING "IN THE GROOVE"

Golf, like life, must be played in the present—you cannot change the past or control the future.
Dean Reinmuth

When golfers are swinging well they often refer to it as being "in the groove." Unfortunately, keeping your swing consistently in the groove is difficult, which is why you may see a tour player get hot for a period of weeks, then suddenly seem to drop out of sight for a while.

It's impossible to stay in the groove all the time. Golf is a constant cycle of finding it, then losing it, finding it, then losing it. The key to playing consistently well is to be able to catch yourself before you get too far out of sync. That way, you'll only need a slight adjustment to get your swing back instead of a major overhaul. You have to expect you'll fall out of the groove sometimes. It's inevitable with even the best swings.

The players most prone to falling out of the groove are the ones who focus on specific body movements (such as "turn the left shoulder under the chin"), because they eventually become inclined to exaggerate those specific feelings, separating them from the feeling of the swing as a whole. That's why you should focus on the movement of the clubhead instead of your body. The feeling of the clubhead is more natural and consistent, and lasts from the start of the swing until the finish, not just for a brief portion of the swing.

The most common pitfall that throws players' swings out of whack is the desire to gain more distance. Unfortunately, players who are playing well begin to think they ought to be able to hit it "just a little farther." In their quest to swing faster, they end up destroying their swing's rhythm and smoothness.

Even if you don't focus on body movements or aren't greedy for distance, you'll still fall out of the groove once in a while.

THE THREE A'S: AWARENESS, ASSESSMENT, ADJUSTMENT

To maintain your swing, you should always be applying the three A's to it: awareness, assessment and adjustment. Combined, they constitute a simple thought process that will save you a lot of time and frustration when it comes to troubleshooting.

AWARENESS

Your "awareness" is your ability to sense what's happening when you swing or play a particular shot. Awareness also pertains to how aware or "in-tune" you are when it comes to planning shots, monitoring your fundamentals, handling specific playing conditions and dealing with your emotions. You need to be aware of whether your practice swing feels good and whether you used that feeling over the ball (in the beginning it may be hard to tell; if so, it's a clue you were ball-focused). If it changed over the ball, you need to be aware of how it felt — was it faster, tighter, less smooth, etc. It's important that you be specific about identifying the problem. I work regularly with a Japanese touring pro whose awareness was very low when we first got started — when I first asked him how he was hitting the ball, all he said was "terrible."

"What do you mean, terrible?" I asked.

"Just what I said — terrible," he answered. I taught him that he had to zero in on precisely what made things "terrible" if he wanted to be able to figure out how to help himself. Did his swing feel jerky or ball-focused? Could he sense the clubhead? What did his shots look like? The more specific you get, the more clues you'll have to help find the answer to the problem.

ASSESSMENT

If you recognize you're having a recurring problem, "assessment" is your ability to figure out what's causing it, how the feeling differs from what a good swing feels like. I say "recurring" because you should only move to the assessment stage when a pattern of two or three bad shots has occurred — not after a single, isolated one. That's because everyone, even a tour pro, will make a poor swing once in a while. You're human, not a machine. Also, a poor shot may be the result of playing conditions, like a poor lie or strong wind.

However, if a pattern of poor shots should occur, such as three consecutive sliced drives, it's obvious you've got more than a random glitch in your swing. If that's the case, it's time to assess the situation.

Don't fall into the trap of judging your shots only by whether you hit them solidly and straight. That may sound like a ridiculous statement, because what more could you ask for but solid, straight shots? The reason I make it is because a common mistake among amateurs is to accidentally allow their alignment to slip out of position so that they're aiming to the right of the target, and then unconsciously correcting their forward-swing path to redirect the shot toward the target. Although the shots they hit are still solid and heading toward the target, the misalignment will eventually cause problems. To avoid this, check yourself periodically by laying a pointer club on the ground during practice.

Also, you shouldn't be satisfied solely because you're making solid contact. You may not be reaching your potential in clubhead speed. I've had many students come to me who, despite tense, jerky swings, learned to manipulate the club squarely back to the ball. But although they were able to make solid contact and hit straight shots, they were nowhere close to achieving their potential in distance or consistency.

Assessment is extremely important. A misdiagnosis of a problem can lead to more trouble. When assessing a bad shot pattern, zero in on four areas:

1. The feeling of the swing. Was it smooth and free, or tight, jerky and/or impact-focused?
2. The feeling of contact. Did you hit the ball fat, thin, toward the heel or toward the toe?
3. The shape of the shot. Was it pushed, pulled, left-to-right, right-to-left, high or low? If it curved, did it bend hard or gently?
4. Your emotions. Your emotions can force you into a pattern of poor swings. It's not unusual to see a player pull three shots in a row while playing a long par five that's bordered all the way up the right side by water. He makes a less-than-good swing because he's worried about losing the ball to the right.

Try to recognize instances in which your emotions are dictating poor swings. Most people don't realize how much their emotions affect their ability to play. Usually, golfers will blame their failures on poor technique or some outside influence, when in fact it may have been their emotions that were the cause. If you've ever mishit a critical shot and then blamed it on the lie, you probably knew deep down that it wasn't the lie, but your nervousness about hitting that particular shot.

When I was younger and playing in competition, the last thing I wanted to believe was that my problems were caused by poor focus or lack of trust.

A closing thought on assessment: Don't expect you'll be able to correctly assess every problem you run into right away. Sometimes you'll experience a glitch that will leave you stumped for a long while. When that happens, your best bet is to go back to the beginning.

First, review your fundamentals. Next, go back to a short, slow swing with a short shaft, teeing the ball up if you want. Work your way through each swing factor — clubhead rotation, downswing angle, etc. By the process of elimination you'll eventually detect where the fault lies.

ADJUSTMENT

After becoming aware of the problem and assessing it, it's time to make the proper adjustments. Usually, the problem can be traced to the tension-related loss of smoothness, rhythm and flow of the motion. But this isn't always the case.

KNOWLEDGE AND EXPERIENCE COUNT HEAVILY TOWARD GOOD ASSESSMENT

As you've probably guessed, how well you are able to assess and adjust depends a lot on your technical knowledge — i.e., the more you know about engines and how they work, the better able you'll be to fix one if it breaks down. The same idea applies to your swing.

Past experiences are often helpful. Typically, most players will have a specific bad habit that recurs from time to time. Because we are creatures of habit, we tend to fall back into the same patterns without realizing it. In my case, I often allow my swing to become too upright and my downswing angle to become too steep. The result is that I hit the ball a little heavy with my irons, costing me distance and control. When that happens, I can quickly assess what's wrong, thanks to past experience, then make an adjustment to my downswing angle.

Making an adjustment isn't always that simple and easy, however. Often, you may have to make more than one or combine two or more. For example, a student of mine once had three she needed to make. One, her alignment was off because she was aiming to the right. Two, she was swinging the club on an outside-in forward-swing path. And three, she was blocking her release at impact. The resulting shots were weak pull-slices. The adjustments she needed to make were first to get properly aligned; second, to trap a forward-swing path that was more from the inside; and third, to exaggerate the feeling of her release so it occurred sooner and blended more with her forward swing.

TIPS FOR MAKING FASTER, BETTER ADJUSTMENTS

SLOW DOWN TO GET IN SYNC

To successfully make a swing change, you have to be able to feel the difference between what you have been doing and what you want to be doing. To best do that, your senses have to be sharp. Unfortunately, most casual players don't have a great deal of swing awareness because they are so ball-focused.

You'll be able to make adjustments much more quickly by focusing on what you feel. You can regain your swing fastest by slowing down your motion. Speed makes it harder to feel or see the subtle movements or flaws which can go undetected when you swing at full speed. The phrase "the hand is quicker than the eye" refers to the fact that when a motion reaches a certain speed, it becomes too fast for the eye to follow. Similarly, if you're trying to learn a foreign language, you'll find it difficult to hear and register the nuances of each word if they're spoken too quickly. You learn by first hearing them slowly, then repeating the words slowly. Once you've learned them, you can increase the pace at which you pronounce them until you reach normal speed. The same principle applies to the swing: Slow it down to increase your feel and awareness for what's happening. If you assess that an adjustment is needed, make it at a slower speed, then gradually increase the pace until you've reached your normal full-swing speed.

REPLACING AN OLD FEELING WITH A NEW ONE

As you've learned here, to hit the ball consistently well, it's crucial to focus on your swing feelings. To make an adjustment, try focusing on replacing an old feeling with a new one.

Sometimes, however, your feelings may be fickle; they can trick you — you may feel that your body is doing one thing, but in fact it's doing another. For example, it may feel as if you're swinging the club back so the shaft is about three-quarters at the top of your backswing, but in reality it's well past the point of being parallel to the ground. If that happens, you'll have to exaggerate the feeling of making a very short swing in order to stop at the point where the shaft is actually at three-quarters.

On the other hand, your feel can be out of touch in the other direction, too, so the length of your swing is actually shorter than you think it is.

Whatever it is, the point is that you often need to exaggerate a feeling in order to implement a specific adjustment, because what feels "normal" to you may not necessarily be correct. It's important that you trust the new feeling over the old one, even if the new one feels odd, unusual, exaggerated or not like your normal swing. Because if your shots are good, then whatever you're doing is correct — even if it feels unusual or "not normal."

The more skilled the player, the closer his feelings reflect what's actually occurring, generally because better players are more swing-focused and shot-focused than ball-focused. The more you use this approach in play and practice, the better in touch you'll get with your clubhead motion. You'll have the most trouble when you're out of touch with any of the six major swing feelings, since they have the most influence over distance and direction.

After assessing the problem, make the adjustment by retrapping what's correct and trusting the new feeling over the old one.

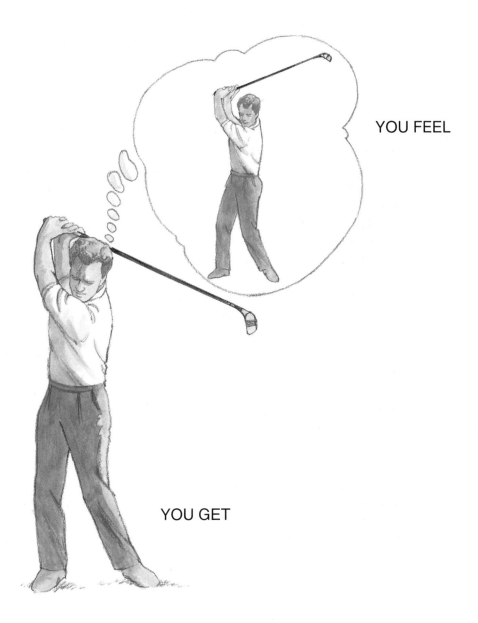

YOU FEEL

YOU GET

Often, a golfer's feelings aren't in sync with what's actually happening in the swing. What you feel is not what you're doing. The first step is to make your rehearsal swing identical to your ball swing (length, speed and clubhead release).

PROCEED BY DEGREES

When your swing gets out of kilter, you'll no doubt quickly get tired of seeing the same bad shot over and over, whether it's a slice, hook or whatever. The natural reaction is to want to make a single, quick adjustment that will immediately return you to hitting the ball straight again.

You'll have better luck if you work in small degrees, and make gradual adjustments in an effort to hit the ball "a little straighter, a little straighter" each time until you've straightened your shots out as much as you want. By proceeding gradually you'll develop a better sense of feel for what's happening during your swing. That will serve you well if you should encounter that particular problem again. For example, if you're slicing badly and you assess the problem as not releasing the clubhead soon enough on the forward swing, then you should start adjusting by focusing on feeling the clubhead release just a little sooner on the forward swing. Each time you make such an adjustment, you should see some change in the ball flight, even if very slight. Keep making slight adjustments in the feeling of the release until your shots have straightened out.

VISUALIZE THE CHANGE

It often helps to imagine yourself making the adjustment you desire. If you've been overswinging and want to adjust so that you stop the club-shaft when it is parallel at the top, form a clear picture in your mind of yourself performing your new swing. "Seeing" it and feeling it at the same time will help make the adjustment happen faster. That's why it's helpful to watch your reflection whenever you can.

When you're trying to make an adjustment to correct a swing fault, it's best to work gradually, in small degrees.

13

FINESSE:
THE KEY TO SHOTMAKING

A golfer is like an artist:
    The sky is his canvas,
    The ball is his paint, and
    The club is his brush.
    Each shot is a new painting.
                  Dean Reinmuth

Good players are good shotmakers. They can "work the ball," make shots curve right or left or fly high or low, depending on the situation. To become a good shotmaker, you need finesse — a fine degree of control over the speed, path, downswing angle and rotation of the clubhead.

When I think about shotmaking, I imagine the sky as a painter would a canvas, with the shot I want to hit being a sweep of brilliant color I want to paint across it. To create a particular shot, or color, I have a palette of primary colors, which are actually various swing feelings. By mixing those feelings together I can create the particular shot I'm seeking to "paint the sky" with — high fades, low draws, etc. It is impossible to tell you exactly how much of each "color" you'll need to mix with another to obtain the specific shot you're looking for. Instead, you have to experiment, as you did when you learned to swing, to find out what specific combinations result in different shots.

THE VALUE OF SHOTMAKING

Players who are adept at working the ball can elude obstacles other players can't. They also can avoid potential trouble because they have the ability to aim away from hazards. For example, if a pond closely hugs the right side of a green, a player who can work the ball both ways will be able to safely aim to the left side of the green, away from the trouble, and fade the ball back toward the pin.

The player who is limited to hitting only a right-to-left shot will have

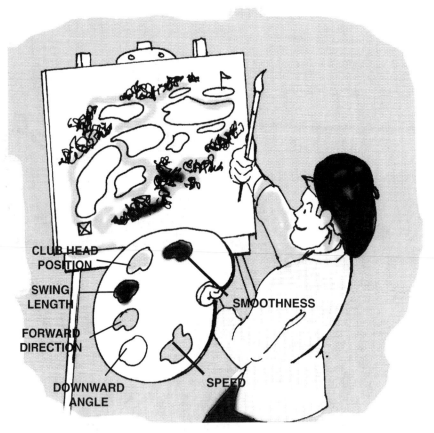

CLUB HEAD
POSITION

SWING
LENGTH

FORWARD
DIRECTION

DOWNWARD
ANGLE

SMOOTHNESS

SPEED

Once you've learned the six major swing feelings, you must
learn how to blend them together to paint pictures of your shots.

to aim out over the water — if he wants to try to land the ball near the
flag — and that's extremely risky business.

It's also good to know how to work the ball because shots that curve
different ways have characteristics other than direction. Left-to-right
shots tend to fly higher and stop faster upon landing, which is why players
who have control problems usually like to hit fades. The opposite is true
with right-to-left shots, which tend to fly lower and run farther upon
landing. That's why this shot-shape is favored by shorter hitters in search
of added distance.

Mastering golf to a high degree requires the ability to hit many different kinds of shots. I'll sometimes ask my students what their definition is

You should practice working the ball under, over and around obstacles. This practice will give you a much better chance of saving strokes when you play.

of a perfect shot. The usual answer is something like "a shot that flies straight and travels the exact distance desired." Wrong. There is no single perfect shot pattern; instead, there are a wide variety of shot patterns. Any one of them may be perfect, depending on the situation.

Sometimes a low, screaming slice or a duckhook is the perfect shot, if you happen to be in a position where you need one to get around a tree. To be the best player you can, you'll need to be able to play an arsenal of shots to fit the many different situations you're liable to face during a round.

Making shots curve is a matter of putting different types and amounts of sidespin on the ball by making certain adjustments to your swing. To make shots fly higher or lower, you need to adjust to change the effective loft of the club you're using and change your downswing angle. It really isn't difficult, and will definitely increase your ability to score.

YOUR NATURAL SHOT PATTERN VS. MANUFACTURED SHOTS

Each player has what's known as a "natural" shot pattern, which is the direction his shots curve when he sets up squarely and makes a normal swing. Almost every golfer can be classified as either a left-to-right player or a right-to-left player. (Occasionally you'll find someone who hits the ball dead straight, but that's extremely rare.)

Obviously, we all feel more comfortable using our natural shot as much as possible, because it's easy. We don't have to make any adjustments or do anything other than swing normally.

You don't have to learn to work the ball to play decently and enjoy the game, but I highly recommend learning how, not only because it will help you score better, but also because it will help heighten your feel for the clubhead in general; and finally because it's extremely satisfying to attempt to create a shot and then be successful.

Learning shotmaking is not as difficult as you might think. Basically, it's a matter of understanding what affects ball flight and how the six major swing factors dictate its characteristics. It's very easy to learn how to impart the types and amounts of sidespin that will make the ball curve in different directions in ranging degrees, and how to change the effective loft of the club and your downswing angle to make the ball fly higher or lower.

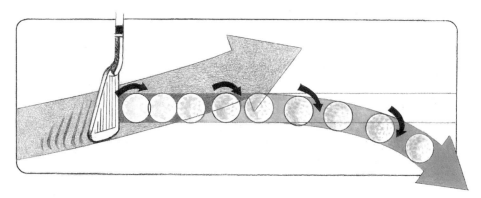

Clockwise sidespin (top), which causes a shot to curve from left to right, is imparted when contact is made while the clubface is open in relation to the line the clubhead is traveling on.

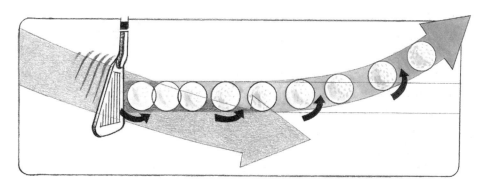

Counterclockwise spin (bottom), which causes a shot to curve from right to left, is imparted when contact is made while the clubface is closed in relation to the line the clubhead is traveling on.

BENDING THE BALL LEFT OR RIGHT

Sidespin is what makes a shot curve. A pitcher intentionally puts sidespin on a baseball when he throws a curveball. A little sidespin equals a little curve, a lot of sidespin equals a lot of curve. You will almost always end up putting a little sidespin on the ball at impact, causing the shot to draw or fade. This sidespin is imparted because the clubface is either slightly open (imparting clockwise spin, causing a fade) or closed (imparting counterclockwise spin, causing a draw) in relation to the line the club-head is traveling on.

The swing factor that affects sidespin and shot direction the most is clubhead rotation. To intentionally change the amount of the sidespin for the purposes of shotmaking, you should focus only on making the adjustments needed to have an open or closed clubface at impact. To adjust the angle of the clubface through impact, exaggerate the feeling of the rotation of the clubhead one way or the other. If you want the face to be closed through impact to impart right-to-left spin, you need to create the feeling the release is occurring sooner in the forward swing. The sooner the release occurs, the more the ball will curve.

If you want the face to be open through impact, imparting left-to-right spin, you need to intentionally delay the rotation of the clubhead on the forward swing. The best way to do that is by keeping your wrists slightly firmer as you swing the club through impact. The more curve you

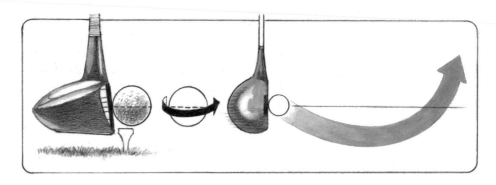

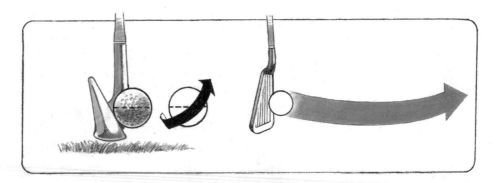

It's easier to put sidespin on the ball with straight-faced clubs (top) because they make contact closer to the ball's equator, while lofted clubs (bottom) make contact closer to the underside of the ball, creating more backspin than sidespin.

want, the firmer your wrists should be (be careful not to take this too far, though, since the extreme will result in a shank).

When you practice working the ball in different directions, it's best to make things easy at first by teeing the ball up and by swinging slowly. That will make it easier for you to sense the rotation of the clubhead, because instead of feeling the clubhead hit the ground, you'll be able to feel the weight and position of the toe of the clubhead turn over.

WHICH CLUBS ARE EASIEST TO BEND

With sidespin, no shot will spin completely horizontally because every clubface is angled upward (some more than others). Therefore, the ball spins on a slanted angle. The closer you can get the ball to spinning horizontally, the more it will curve. That's why you'll be able to work the ball to the right or left much easier with straight-faced clubs like medium irons, long irons and woods. The straighter the face, the closer you'll make contact to the ball's equator; and the closer you make contact to the ball's equator, the closer you'll get to horizontal sidespin, equaling more curve.

Conversely, a shallow-faced club makes contact more toward the underside of the ball, beneath the equator, so you'll get closer to perfectly vertical spin (backspin), and thus less curve. That's why it's extremely difficult to hit a big hook or slice with a wedge or nine iron.

HIGH BALLS AND LOW BALLS

To hit a ball higher or lower than usual, you need to make adjustments to increase or decrease the effective loft of the club and adjust your downswing angle.

For higher-than-normal shots, you needs to increase the loft of the club, so you should play the ball about an inch ahead of normal while keeping your hands in the same place. This will tilt the face back a little bit, adding loft.

Then, rather than hitting down on the ball on a steep angle, you need to swing the club forward on a slightly "up and under" angle, creating a feeling used when you need to get a shot over a tree. Combined, these adjustments will cause the ball to rise more quickly and fly higher than usual. Take care, however, that the combination of playing the ball forward and making a more upward forward swing doesn't result in your hitting behind the ball. Also, note that it's easiest to "lift" the ball up more quickly from a cushiony lie.

To hit a shot lower than usual, play the ball about an inch farther back in your stance while again leaving your hands in the same place as usual; doing so will tilt the face forward a little, taking some of the loft away. Also, put a touch more of your weight on your left side and set your left hip and shoulder slightly lower than the right, then swing the club back and forward on a steeper downswing angle than usual. The ball will fly low and run hard.

DON'T FORGET SMOOTHNESS

When you try to manufacture a specific type of shot, you're creating swings that are a little out of the ordinary. That often causes players to force certain movements and become either hesitant or quick. That's the main reason why casual golfers often have trouble successfully working the ball. Remember, although you may need to adjust some of the six major swing factors to "create" a certain type of shot, one of them must *always* remain the same, and that's smoothness. That's why your best swings always feel smooth.

The best way to develop your shotmaking abilities is to build confidence through practice. Get out on the range and experiment to find out what kinds of different shots you can hit. I always find it interesting and a lot of fun to see just what I can make the ball do. To me, practicing shotmaking can add a lot of life to what might be an otherwise dull practice session. As you learn to hit different shots, remember not only the adjustments you made, but the feelings they produced. The feeling of the clubhead moving inside-out or outside-in, the feeling of the rotation of the clubhead through impact, etc. Recalling these feelings later will help you reproduce that shot when it's needed on the course.

BE CREATIVE AND PAINT THE SKY

Once you've had some luck teaching yourself to work the ball from side to side and up and down, mix things up and try to combine high and low

Be creative and paint the sky when you practice.

trajectories with your curveballs. Try to paint the sky with as many kinds of shots as possible. Remember, the more shots you can play, the more weapons you'll have to attack the course.

14

RECALLING A GOOD SWING

If I'da cleared the trees and drove the green, it would'a been a great tee shot.

Sam Snead

In golf, you need to be able to make the best possible swing whenever you step up to a ball, but that's not always easy. That's especially true during a weekend round when you may have to wait at least five minutes between shots. When the time finally comes to play, you face the pressure of a possible penalty if you don't hit the ball well. I mentioned early in this book how important it is to trust in your ability. Trust puts your emotional side at ease, leaving you free to perform without doubts, reservations or inhibitions. However, I've found that trust is not built easily in most players.

Even if we possess the technical ability to hit certain types of shots, we still don't always trust ourselves to perform them well. Instead, we doubt ourselves, especially on the course.

Think about it: How many times have you failed to execute a certain shot, knowing full well you've done it several times before, that you have the ability? You might even drop a second ball and hit that one perfectly, which compounds your frustration. It happens to everyone, and it's one of the most exasperating things about the game — when you fail to make a good swing, even though you know full well that you're capable.

Why can't we hit our best shots more often on our first attempt? The truth is, we can. The key lies in how we prepare ourselves to hit the ball. Stored within every golfer's mind are a number of "files," each representing what it feels like to hit a different type of shot: drives, long irons, pitches, chips, fades, draws, sand shots, lag putts, etc. When you need to play a specific shot, you call up that "feeling file" which has all the information you need — the club needed, any swing adjustments that need to be made, and most important, what it *feels* like to hit that particular shot.

You started creating "feeling files" the first day you began learning to play. Your first file was probably how to grip the club. You tried to remember how your fingers were positioned on the club, how it felt to hold the grip in your hands. You stored that in your memory, and the next time you practiced, you tried to recall all those feelings. Each time you practiced it became easier to recall that information, until you eventually didn't even have to think about it consciously. Instead, you reached a point where your hands seemed to automatically wrap around the club in perfect position. You were able to reach that point because your memory locked on to what it felt like when your hands were on the club properly. From then on, you put your hands on the club and were only satisfied that your grip was correct when it *felt* right to you. If it felt wrong, you rearranged your fingers until you arrived at what you perceived as the correct feeling.

The ability to remember and reproduce a feeling — good grip or how it feels to hit a certain type of shot — is the secret to performing consistently well. You've probably had the experience of stepping up to a shot and, for some reason, knowing beforehand you were going to hit it well. You weren't sure why, but you just had a good feeling. Then, boom, you hit a good shot. Other times you step up to the ball feeling like you're going to hit a bad shot. When that happens, nine times out of ten, you hit it badly. Therefore, it's crucial to focus on recalling good feelings before you hit the ball. Then trust those feelings to trigger a good swing.

PRACTICE YOUR RECALL

The more you work at recalling your good feelings in practice, the easier it will be to recall them when you're on the course. At the range, work first at finding a good swing feeling, then purposely take a break. Then try to recall that feeling again. That sounds simple, but it's not.

I had a student once who was a chronic slicer. And his tee shots were very short. During his first lesson his primary goal was to learn to draw the ball to get more distance. After we worked on making his swing smoother and refining his release, he was hitting the ball straighter and farther, but his shots were still fading slightly from left-to-right. Because he wanted badly to draw the ball, I helped him adjust his feeling of release until he hit a right-to-left shot. He hit ten balls in a row, all with perfect, gentle draws. His face lit up with a smile.

"All right," I said. "Now hit a fade for me."

His smiled disappeared. "No!" he said, shaking his head vehemently. "If I do that, I'll lose the feeling of what it's like to hit this wonderful draw, and if that happens, I may not be able to find it again!"

I explained that the more he purposely tried to forget a feeling and then regain it, the better he would become at regaining it in the future. Plus, once that happened there would be less of a chance he'd lose it and never find it again.

It's like traveling from one place to another. The more times you make the trip, the deeper the route becomes etched into your memory until sooner or later you could find your way without the need of a map or directions.

If you wait too long between trips, though, you may forget how to get there and will need help finding your way.

It's like a filing cabinet: If you haphazardly throw all your information into a big drawer or had someone else file your information, and suddenly you needed to find a document, it would take a long time to locate it. You must train yourself to organize and clearly define your swing feelings.

There are two specific exercises I prescribe that will sharpen your ability to call up a good swing. In practice, most players need to hit a number of balls before their swing begins to feel good and their shots are accurate. As soon as you find the feeling, *stop*. Instead of continuing to hit balls, take a short break. Then go back and try to find that feeling again. As you get better at relocating the feeling, make your breaks longer. This exercise is valuable because it duplicates what happens on the course, where you hit a shot then have to wait a few minutes before hitting the next. Remember, though, to only focus on how your good swings feel and forget the bad. This is called positive response recall.

When practicing shotmaking, as soon as you've got the feel for hitting a particular shot, say a draw, jump to a different one, like a fade. Stay with the fade until you're hitting that well, then go back and try to relocate the feeling of the draw. Again, the idea is not to dwell on a particular feeling, but instead to practice abandoning it and relocating it, so that on the course you'll be able to relocate the feeling more easily when you need it.

You may not find these exercises a lot of fun at first. Most golfers don't like the idea of abandoning a good feeling. But I guarantee they will build your ability to call up a good swing on the course. Generally, less skilled players should practice for a short period, say five or ten minutes, then take a short break, say about one minute. Players with more advanced skills, on the other hand, should take breaks of about two or three minutes and longer.

Your rehearsal (practice) swing plays a key role in helping you relocate good feelings because it gives you feedback before you hit the shot. Make a rehearsal swing that feels exactly like what you want as your "ball swing;" the next thing you should do is to immediately step up to the ball and repeat that same swing, that same feeling, without changing it.

THE ROLE OF VISUALIZATION IN RECALLING A GOOD SWING

You hear a lot about how important visualization is when it comes to playing golf, how essential it is to picture the shot you want to hit before you play it. Why? So you can, by remembering what the shot looks like, also conjure up the feeling of what it's like to hit it. When you imagine a nice juicy hamburger, you remember not only what it looks like, but also what it smells and tastes like.

When you imagine a shot, you also remember what it sounded like and felt like to hit it, along with the visual image. Remember the good feelings and you'll increase your chances of creating them again.

A gentleman I met once named Doc Maynard was having trouble understanding why he could be cruising along and playing well, then suddenly lose his good swing feelings and not be able to get them back. "I'll be negotiating the course with no trouble, hitting good shots," he said, "then suddenly I won't be able to do anything right." I asked him if he visualized his shots beforehand. He said he planned the shot he wanted to hit, but didn't try to picture it vividly, nor did he make an effort to recall a good swing feeling.

I told him every golfer needs to train himself to recall his best swings, but he seemed puzzled. I said making a good golf swing is like trying to remember someone's name. Sometimes it comes to you easily. Other times you draw a blank. Still other times you may have it on the tip of your tongue.

Recalling something, whether it's a name or a feeling, becomes easier when you associate a visual image with it. To give him an example, I counted to five in Japanese: "Ichi, ne, san, she, go." I did it very quickly

The object behind visualizing a good shot is so that, along with recalling the image, you can at the same time recall the feeling of the good swing that produced it.

though — *ichi-ne-san-she-go* — and then asked him to repeat it. Looking slightly bewildered, he said he couldn't. I repeated the words, but this time I slowed down and separated them, giving him a visual image for each sound: For ichi, which is pronounced "itchy," I scratched my arm; for ne, pronounced "knee," I pointed to my kneecap; for "san," I told him to think of the sun; etc. By the end of dinner he had learned the phrase completely.

I told him he would need to review the sounds and images often over the next several days, though, if he wanted to commit them to memory. I told him he could apply the same recall method to his golf game by associating the visual images of his good shots with the feelings he experienced when he hit them.

(Incidentally, over a year went by before I happened to run into Doc again. He looked at me and said, "I can't remember your name, but I do remember 'ichi-ne-san-she-go!'" Maybe I should have taught him to remember my name, instead!)

VISUALIZATION MUST BE BACKED WITH TECHNICAL KNOWLEDGE

For visualization to do you any good, you need to already have the proper technical knowledge and acquired ability to hit the specific shot. Simply imagining a shot won't allow you to hit it. I can visualize somebody typing, and I can sit down and strike keys on a typewriter, but that doesn't give me the fundamental and technical knowledge of where each key is, nor the coordination skills necessary to type correctly. Likewise, a beginner may be able to swing a golf club back and forth, but if he has not acquired the knowledge of the six major swing factors and what they feel like, then he won't be able to hit good shots, even if he visualizes them.

You may have heard it said that a good imagination can help you when it comes to playing out of trouble. That's true, but again, it won't particularly help you play a shot you've never tried before. But practicing your ability to imagine will allow you to dream up ways to get out of trouble, ways less imaginative players might not be able to think of.

NEGATIVE VISUALIZATION

Beware that, just as visualizing a good shot can provoke good feelings, visualizing a bad shot can just as easily provoke bad feelings. Sometimes you can't help but imagine a poor result, especially in a pressure situation. Your mind is flooded with images of what you fear — the ball dropping into water or a bunker, or lipping out of the cup. The fear these images create causes tension that keeps you from performing well. If your dominant visual image is a negative one, you'll probably be beaten before you start. (Remember I mentioned that back in my competitive playing days I was haunted by images of duckhooks whenever I pulled out my driver? Sometimes I could overcome them, but often I couldn't.)

Bad shot patterns and bad visual images become a vicious cycle. If, for example, you're topping your fairway woods, when you try to hit your three wood you'll tend to remember all those topped shots, and the fear of hitting another one will spring to mind. This streak of bad images can be difficult to break. Normally, you can't break out of it by forcing yourself to visualize a good shot, because it's either a technical problem that's causing the bad shots or poor focus. The solution is to go to the range and work out the technical problem or redevelop the proper focus. Once you're hitting good shots again, you'll be able to use the positive visual images and a positive cycle of good memories to spark good results.

When a negative image imposes, it doesn't do any good to try to crowd it out with positive verbal commands. Instead, let the image play out in vivid detail. Then tell yourself, "There, that's what I *don't* want to do, and here's what I *do* want to do." Then visualize the good result, make a practice swing to reinforce a positive feeling and, without further hesitation, hit the shot. By confronting the negative image you'll get it out of your system, clearing the way for a positive image.

IMPROVING YOUR ABILITY TO VISUALIZE

Some people are naturally adept at visualizing, at picturing a positive image and at the same time calling up the good feeling associated with it. If you aren't good at it, you can acquire the skill by practicing.

A great way to improve your visualization is to try to execute different short wedge shots, each time imagining a picture of exactly what you want to do. Hit high flop shots, then low one-bouncers, sixty-yard shots, then forty-yard shots. Work on tying in what you visualize with what you feel — if you hit the shot a little too hard or soft, make an adjustment. Remember, the idea isn't just to visualize, but to associate a good feeling with the image. When you change the image in your mind, your swing feeling should change with it.

VISUALIZATION AND PRESSURE

When there's pressure on you to perform well, the ability to imagine and remember a past positive performance will be extremely valuable toward calming your emotions. By doing that, you remind yourself that on the trust ladder you've successfully ascended to a certain level. In other words, you've done it before, so you can do it again. On the 72nd hole of the 1992 Players Championship, Davis Love III was in the lead when he pushed his tee shot into the right rough on the par-four 18th, leaving him with a long iron to the green and trouble both left and right. As he readied to hit, Johnny Miller, one of the television announcers, pointed out that Love was most likely trying to think of a similar situation where he'd hit a good shot. The resulting smooth swing produced a beautiful four iron that landed in the middle of the green and rolled to fifteen feet, from where Davis two-putted for victory.

CREATING NEW FEELING FILES

Whenever you hit a good shot, your work isn't over after the ball has been struck. It's important to watch the shot until it lands, then take a couple of seconds to focus on what just happened and what it felt like so you can store it in your memory. If you want, make another practice swing and try to repeat that feeling again. The better you ingrain the memory of a good shot, the better your chances will be of recalling it completely at a later time.

When practicing on the range, take your time between shots. Focus on the feeling after a good one. Too often I see players reaching for another ball even though the last shot they hit is still in the air. Instead, feel the shot and relate that feeling to the flight of the ball. On the other hand, if you hit a bad shot, don't even give it a second thought. A negative feeling is nothing you'll want to remember. Only assess a bad shot if it is part of a pattern.

Each time you learn to do something new in golf, you're creating a new feeling file, or memory. Each time you learn to play a new shot, or you successfully execute in a specific situation, make an effort to remember it. When you learn to play a certain shot, you create a file in your mind. If you reach a situation where you need to hit a similar shot, you'll need to call on that memory. So when you try a certain type of shot for the first time and are successful, make sure to dwell on it for a moment afterwards so as to store the memory of how it looked and felt for later use.

UNLIKE A COMPUTER, YOUR MEMORY CAN FADE

In a lot of ways, swinging a golf club is like riding a bike. As with anything, though, you'll get "rusty," forget some of the nuances and will need to be refreshed from time to time. I found that out awhile back when I jumped on a bike for the first time in ten years. I was gliding along fine until I tried to ride "no hands" as I had when I was a kid. Next thing I knew I was almost picking myself and the bike up off the ground. The ins and outs of keeping my balance while my hands were off the handlebars had escaped me, though there was a time when I could do it with ease.

Memories and skills dull with lack of use. I used to experience that every spring when the weather in Illinois got warm enough to play again. Although I tried to stay sharp over the winter, the amount of practicing I could do was extremely limited. As such, I felt there were a lot of things I had to relearn every year.

The first thing I'd do when the range opened was to run through all the different shots I had in my arsenal to refresh my memory of what they felt like.

I'd go to the practice green and hit pitches, chips and putts of all kinds. I wasn't concerned as much with results as I was with getting back in touch with the feelings of each shot. The point is, to call up a good feeling before hitting a shot, that feeling will have to be relatively fresh in your memory (which is why rehearsal swings are so important).

15

BRINGING YOUR SWING TO THE COURSE

If you can't have fun . . . don't play.
Dean Reinmuth

common complaint I hear from average players is that they hit the
ball well on the practice range, but not on the golf course. Think
back to the ultimate goal, way back in Chapter 1, which was to hit
your best shots more often. Hitting your best shots more often on the
range is certainly a good thing, but you probably won't get any real satisfaction until you can do it on the course. In this final chapter we'll explore
some of the reasons you may not swing as well on the course as you'd like,
and some ways to overcome that.

MAINTAINING THE RIGHT ATTITUDE

One reason you may not be playing up to your potential on the course is
that you aren't approaching your shots with the right attitude. Your score
is the sum of its parts, each part being an individual shot. That may sound
like a cliche, but it's no less true. Think of each shot as its own game, and
play one game at a time.

You can't hit two shots at once, only one, so focus only on that one.
Unfortunately, most people approach a shot carrying negative emotions
from their last shot or preoccupied with the shot that's to follow. You'll
never play your best if you dwell on the past or worry about the future.
Focus only on the feeling of the swing at that moment, without trying to
control the outcome of the shot. By focusing on positive swing feelings, I
guarantee you'll hit your best shots more often.

Allowing negative thoughts or doubts to carry over from a poor shot is
common. You'll seldom see pros affected that way. They've learned to put
a poor shot behind them, recompose themselves and focus fully on hit-

ting the next shot well. And believe me, a poor shot can be just as big a blow to a pro's psyche as it is to you, maybe more, since at a pro's level most people believe they aren't supposed to hit any poor shots.

Occasionally, you may blow what you think is an easy shot. Usually this happens because, instead of focusing on it, you assumed it was a done deal and started thinking about the next shot or the next hole. In the third round of the 1992 Los Angeles Open, Fred Couples hit a beautiful pitch to within less than three feet of the pin on his third shot to the par-five 17th. It looked like a gimme, but he missed it. Later, he explained that he'd gotten "a little ahead of himself" and was thinking about the difficult 18th hole, instead of focusing completely on the putt.

I once had a student who told me he had great success pulling off tough shots, but often found himself screwing up easy ones. "I feel like I have a better chance of getting the ball close when I'm playing a tricky cut-lob to a tight pin over a bunker than I do hitting a normal pitch to a big, unprotected green," he complained. The answer was clear: The bigger the challenge he faced, the more focused he became. On easier shots his mind wandered, because he took his performance on them for granted.

HOW TO IMPROVE YOUR FOCUS

Another reason you may not play as well on the course as you think you should is because you aren't able to recall and focus well enough on each individual shot. Instead, you allow yourself to become distracted. It's easier to establish the proper feel on the range because you can hit ball after ball after ball. Your swing feeling stays fresh and easy to recall. And if you mishit a shot, you can make a slight adjustment to the previous swing feeling and test the results right away. Also, you don't have to worry about controlling distance and direction, since there's no penalty for a bad shot.

But during a competitive round, you're forced to spend a lot of "down time" between shots, when your mind can wander. That's okay. Your mind should take a rest between shots. But the better you are able to focus on the shot you're facing, the better you'll be able to execute.

FOCUSING ON THE SHOT AT HAND

When you're well-focused, it's easier to keep your attention on the shot at hand and tune out distractions like noises or movements. Most people who have difficulty focusing allow things — the lie, hazards, playing partners — to distract them.

DIRECTING YOUR FOCUS WITH A PRE-SHOT ROUTINE

A good movie or story draws your focus until it has your complete and undivided attention. You can allow a shot to draw you in the same way, and by following the same pre-shot routine.

A pre-shot routine serves two purposes. One, it helps keep your muscles relaxed. Two, a routine gives you something to focus on and keeps away negative thoughts. At the end of the routine you should be completely focused on executing a good swing. A consistent routine will help you arrive at the same high level of focus every time.

Here's an example of an ideal five-step pre-shot routine:

1. Assess the conditions. How is the lie? How far do you need to hit the shot? Are you hitting to a large or small target? Will the wind affect it? Are there any hazards or obstacles to contend with?

2. Visualize and determine the best shot to play. A draw or fade? High, low or normal trajectory? Does the situation warrant a gamble, or should you play safe?

3. Choose the club. A standard five iron? A small six or a hard seven?

4. Make a rehearsal swing. Make "rehearsal" (practice) swings until you find one that feels good, and that duplicates the feeling of the swing needed to produce the shot you've visualized.

5. Duplicate your rehearsal swing. The next step is to duplicate the rehearsal swing on the ball before you lose the feeling. Try to repeat that swing feeling without shifting your focus to the impact, where you want the ball to go, or any type of verbal command.

This may sound like a lot to do before each shot, but once you get into the habit you'll find it goes very quickly, each step flowing into the next. If you move through the routine briskly, you'll find distractions much less likely to creep into your mind before you swing. For example, as soon as you make a practice swing that feels good, immediately repeat that feeling over the ball while the feeling is fresh in your mind. That's why it's important to align your body *before* the practice swing. That way you can immediately step up and swing at the ball once you've found the right feeling.

Each step in the pre-shot routine is important, but if there's one you should pay particular attention to, it would be the practice swing. Yet this is the one thing many golfers leave out of their preparation.

The practice swing is your reference point. On the range, the last ball you hit can be a reference point.

On the course, make a rehearsal swing and use it as a reference point. Was it good or not so good? Rehearse your swing until one feels right — smooth, controlled, balanced, the correct speed and length — then step up to the ball and duplicate that swing. You won't be slowing up play by rehearsing your swing a couple of times to find your best feeling. The more you do it, the quicker you'll be able to trust yourself to find the feeling you're looking for. Personally, I don't care for slow play. But I'd rather play with someone who takes an extra few seconds to make a practice swing and then follows it with a good shot than someone who doesn't take a practice swing and then knocks the ball in the woods.

It's extremely important to step up to the ball and duplicate a good practice swing immediately. Too many people lose the swing feeling just before they hit the shot because they become focused on the ball or they allow distracting thoughts or commands to creep in.

I once had a student who, despite having developed a good swing and a decent short game, complained he couldn't score lower than the mid-80s. The reason was because he deliberated too long before hitting his shots. He would give himself verbal commands — "do this, don't do that" — which hurt more than helped his ability to perform. He was thinking instead of feeling. He also was overtrying. His breakthrough came when he and a friend found themselves in a position where they had to rush in order to complete their final nine holes before darkness. On the front nine he shot his usual 43, but on the back, while making an effort to play at a faster pace, he shot a one-under-par 34. He told me that speeding things up had given him a whole different feeling. "Normally, I guess you'd say I'm a slow player," he said. "I usually take a lot of time trying to make sure I've thought of everything and, in effect, I guess I try too hard. But when we were trying to beat the sunset, I knew I couldn't waste time, and I got into a rhythm of going through my pre-shot routine briskly and then immediately hitting the shot. I started to get this sort of carefree feeling whenever I stepped to the ball that, okay, I've done everything I can to prepare, and now all I can do is make the best swing I can — if it's a good shot, great; if it's not, it's not.

"I approached everything that way — drives, approaches, chips, putts — and I hit everything better than usual. I even pitched close to the hole on the 18th and sunk the four-footer to save par when I knew I needed it to finish one under par. Normally I would've been more nervous about that, but I kept the same brisk rhythm between my pre-shot routine and hitting the shot, and never gave myself a chance to think too much, overtry or go blank. And the results were terrific."

This gentleman learned three things from his experience. The first was that he had been getting in his own way by thinking conscious thoughts before he swung. By playing faster shots that day, he hit shots before he had a chance to interfere with himself. The results were dramatically better.

Second, he found that a more carefree attitude worked a lot better than his too serious one. He stopped worrying so much about the results. Doing that helped him hit better shots. Sometimes, the more you want something and the harder you press to get it, the harder it is to attain. By relaxing, it often becomes easier to grasp.

Third, he discovered that better golf occurs when you think less and rely a lot more on feelings.

Take a lesson from the above story and realize all you can really do before any shot is to prepare as well as possible, then hit the ball. Visualize the shot and recall your best feeling with your practice swing, then duplicate that practice swing feeling over the ball. Wherever the ball goes from there, it goes; you've done the best you can and can't ask anymore of yourself. As Bobby Jones' teacher Stewart Maiden used to say, "Just hit the shot; it's got to go somewhere."

The first step in your pre-shot routine should be to assess the conditions, determine what kind of shot you want to play and choose the club you want to use.

Second, visualize the shot and recall the good swing feeling associated with it.

Third, align yourself to the target line, just to the side of the ball.

Fourth, make rehearsal swings until you find the right swing feeling.

Fifth, move up to the ball without hesitation and duplicate your rehearsal swing feeling over the ball.

AVOID STEERING

It's easier to swing freely on the practice range because there isn't rough or trees or sand or water for the ball to land in. When presented with obstacles of this kind on the course, players tend to "steer" the ball to the target by guiding the clubhead instead of swinging it. Steering is manipulation that stems from a lack of trust in the motion of your swing, and will hamper your accuracy rather than help it. Only by letting go will you be able to achieve proper clubhead rotation, forward-swing path and downswing angle, all of which combine to result in an accurate shot.

Even good players will succumb to steering once in a while. When you feel yourself wanting to guide the club, make sure to keep your practice swing loose and to maintain that feeling when you hit the ball. Focus on the feeling of the clubhead flowing past the ball and into the *finish*, not on the impact or on the result of the shot.

It will also help, when faced with a steering situation, to back down and play to the fattest part of the green, or take less club off the tee. You aren't being defensive by doing this, but instead are giving yourself more of a chance to make a free, offensive swing and are avoiding the urge to manipulate or steer the clubhead. If you think about it, one of the easiest shots in golf is when you lay up with an iron on your second shot to a par five. Why? Because you have a generous target — the fairway — and you don't have to worry about hitting the ball a long way. Your goal is only to move it far enough to allow yourself a shot at the green with your third shot. Consequently, most people hit this shot — the lay-up on a par five — very well because there is no need to press or steer. If you can make that same swing when hitting to a well-guarded target, you'll have a better chance of getting the ball there. Your mind should be focused more on the motion of the swing and less on where the ball is going.

MANAGING YOUR CONFIDENCE

Golf is a game of peaks and valleys. Confidence in your game usually rises and falls as you progress through a given round. Part of your job as a player is to manage your confidence by trying to keep it high when you're on a peak and being able to pull yourself out of a valley when it gets low. For most golfers, confidence is something that's easily lost and often hard to regain. It doesn't take much to shake it (as anyone who has missed two short putts in a row will attest), and it usually takes more than one or two good shots to bring it back.

Your overall confidence level will fluctuate from one day to the next because the way you feel physically will fluctuate. It's difficult to describe, but some days you simply feel better, stronger, more in-tune with your swing and the club than you do on others. Tour pros admit this. Most know that you usually won't find four days in a row during a tournament when you're playing your best. One of those days you'll be a little off your game. Those are the days when you need an excellent short game and a good attitude to get you through and help you post a good score. You can either win a tournament or lose it depending on how you persevere on the off days.

Part of managing your confidence and your game is not to press on days when you don't feel as sharp as usual, when your degree of control over your swing and the ball isn't quite as good as it normally is. Whenever I have a day like that, I do two things. One, I step down one rung on the trust ladder and slow my swing speed down a little, which makes it easier to control. (I always take one more club to compensate for the

HOLE OF TRUST

The more difficult the course or hole, the more you must trust the free motion of the swing into the finish. Start with an easy level course and work your way up the ladder of trust.

slower speed.) That sounds easy, but getting yourself to do it when you're on the course can be difficult — most players want to go full-throttle all the time. It takes discipline to ease back, but it's the intelligent way to play.

Two, I avoid attempting any high-risk shots that will push my emotions to the brink of where they'll interfere with my ability to perform. So if I'm having "one of those days," I probably won't try to reach a par five in two if there's a lot of trouble around the green; instead, I'll lay up and hit a short iron for my third. Not only will I probably keep the ball out of trouble and avoid making a big number, but I also will feel like I'm "playing smart," and that's good for my confidence.

You should take this approach when "the wheels start falling off." It happens to everyone, from amateur to pro, when, during the middle of a round, shots start to go awry and you can't seem to do anything right. Sometimes it happens suddenly, when you have a "blow-up" hole; and sometimes it happens gradually, when you make several bogeys in a row. The fact remains, you've lost control. If that happens, slow down and back down. Focus on making one good swing at a time and you should eventually assume control over your rhythm and your game again.

Think of it this way: When you've got your A swing going during the round, picture and play A type shots. When the momentum changes or you're having an off day, picture and play B or C shots. Forcing A shots when you're playing your B or C game will cause your scores to go up dramatically.

MAKING THE COURSE
A LEARNING PLACE AGAIN

One reason you may not be playing to your potential on the course is that your emotional side is in an uproar because you're viewing the course as a survival place. If that's the case, refer back to Chapter 4 and take steps to turn it into a learning place until you get comfortable with playing for score. Think of it as putting training wheels on your bike again for a little while. Know that in time you'll be able to take them off and proceed confidently without them.

COMPETITIVE PLAY

When you play competitively, you leave yourself open for other people to know how well you performed. It becomes a matter of pride in your own success or failure.

If, like most of us, you get jittery under tournament pressure, your best bet is to go back to the trust ladder and find a rung where you feel comfortable performing competitively. Usually, that's playing a two-dollar Nassau with your friends or playing a course that isn't especially difficult. Step up from there to more organized competitions and tougher courses. You may not feel comfortable right away on the next rung, but be patient — a little nervousness isn't bad. Continue moving upward on the ladder until you've reached the level you want to compete on, but remember to drop back to an easier level to get your confidence back if you feel bogged down at a certain point. Many tour pros do the same thing by gaining competitive experience overseas, on the mini tour or on the Ben Hogan Tour before building the confidence and skills needed to succeed on the regular PGA Tour.

Even when you reach a point where you can perform with relative confidence at a certain level, you still may be confronted from time to time with crucial shots where you are affected by the situation and feel nervous, such as at the end of a match or a sudden-death playoff. If this happens, try to keep your thoughts away from the situation in between shots by focusing on your breathing, a trick that athletes in other sports use. Don't try to control your breathing, instead simply become aware of the smooth pace and rhythm of it — in, out, in, out. Stay focused on your breathing and within a minute or so your mind will calm down.

The amount of pressure you feel at a given time is usually directly related to your desire and your perspective on the game. Playing well and winning means a lot to some people, whether as a sense of accomplishment or as proof of their self-worth. In professional golf, it means the difference between making a fine living and struggling to hold on to your tour card. But if you don't do it for a living, whether it's playing golf, tennis, football or basketball, it's not worth getting too worked up about. And even if it is your career, perspective is in order. In an article in *Golf Magazine*, tour pro Billy Andrade was asked what his thoughts would be if he were facing a three-foot putt to win the U.S. Open. "I'd probably be thinking that there must be about two billion people in the world who didn't care one way or the other whether I made it or not," he answered. That kind of thinking will bring you back to reality fast.

LOOK AHEAD AND BE POSITIVE

One of the big differences between good players and poor players is that good players, when planning a shot, zero in on where they want to hit the ball rather than where they don't want to hit it. Their swing feelings and visual images are almost always slanted toward the positive, which is one of the reasons they score so well. Once they get a good round going, they continue to focus on making good swings and getting positive results. Most amateurs, if they find themselves playing phenomenally well, actually get worried and start anticipating disaster. Or, they stiffen up and try to just get safely back to the clubhouse instead of riding that streak of good play.

Although it's easy to be negative in golf, it's easier than you may think to be positive. Most bad shots can be balanced out by a good recovery, so if you put yourself in a bad position, try to focus on making a good swing on the next shot. If Seve Ballesteros let it bother him every time he hit an errant ball, he wouldn't have won three British Opens and two Masters. The same went for the great Walter Hagen, who was known for both his occasional wildness and his placid ability to bail his ball out of whatever difficulties he'd gotten it into. When asked how he could stay so calm after hitting a rotten shot, he replied, "I fully expect that I will hit several bad shots during the course of a round. So when one occurs, I don't get upset, because I know that that is simply one of them." The Haig realized you couldn't be perfect at golf; it was too demanding a game. He accepted that mistakes would occur, and realized that a negative attitude wouldn't help matters when they did. By taking that same tack, you'll relieve yourself from a lot of self-inflicted pressure.

Accept the fact you won't hit every shot perfectly. Although you need to trust yourself that you can make a good swing, the fact is you won't do it 100 percent of the time because you're human. So when a bad shot happens, accept it as one of the many challenges of the game and give the next one your best effort.

SUMMARY

On Learning:

- Golf is an **acquired skill**. To best acquire it, you need **good information** and an **efficient method of learning.**

- There are two levels of the brain: The **analytical level**, which analyzes and decides, and the **performance level**, which directs the performance of unconscious actions. When you learn to perform something physical, you receive information on the analytical level, which then communicates it to your performance level through visual images, sounds and feelings.

- Learning is a gradual, **step-by-step** process.

- Your golf game is made up of two sides: The **technical side**, which pertains to your knowledge of how to hit the ball, and the **emotional side**, which pertains to your feelings/emotions and whether they are beneficial or detrimental to your ability to perform. Both sides must work in harmony for you to play your best golf.

- You must develop **trust** in your ability in order to play good golf. The opposite of trust is doubt, which undermines performance. Doubt increase tension; trust alleviates it. You must replace doubt with trust in order to improve.

- Your ability to learn will increase in a **learning situation**, which is any situation where you feel calm and an absence of pressure. The opposite is a **survival situation**, which imposes pressure on your ability to perform (for a number of possible reasons), increasing tension and inhibiting learning.

- You can **change a survival situation into a learning situation** by controlling the conditions, i.e., improving your lie if you doubt your ability to play from it. The more you practice in a learning situation, the faster you'll learn.

- **Trapping** is the ability to discover what's technically correct by experimenting between two boundaries (too much … too little), and is essential to teaching yourself how to swing.

- The **trust ladder** is a series of skill levels ranging from easy to hard. You must be able to honestly assess your position on the trust ladder and start from there in order to learn and advance upward. When you experience doubt, you should drop down to a level where you have trust.

- **Learning** will occur more quickly if you relax, stay loose and enjoy the process.

On Tension:

- **Physical tension** is the worst and most common detriment to striking a golf ball well, cutting down on both accuracy and distance. Your swing should be tension-free and should feel relaxed, smooth and effortless, not tight, jerky or hard.

- Focusing on the ball is the major cause of tension in golfers. You are **ball-bound** when the presence of the ball inspires tension in your swing. When you rid your swing of tension, the improvement will be dramatic.

- **Other sources of tension** include competition, playing conditions, verbal commands and habit.

On Building a Tension-Free Swing:

- **Feel** is the smoothness and freedom of the swing.

- **Form** is the combination of body and club movement that gives proper shape to the swing.

- **Finesse** is the ability to control the speed and movement of the clubhead while maintaining freedom.

- **Fundamentals** (grip, posture, stance, etc.) are extremely important, but you are allowed a certain amount of flexibility within them.

- Your **alignment** must be correct. Poor alignment leads to club manipulation and errant shots. Very few amateurs aim properly.

- There are **six key checkpoints** of form that occur throughout the swing — address, halfway back, top, halfway forward, impact and finish. You should monitor them frequently by watching your reflection.

On Developing Feel and Freedom of Motion in Your Swing:

- To build maximum clubhead speed you must employ **centrifugal force** instead of brute force/body effort.

- Brute force and tension decrease motion and will usually lead to one of three poor swing types: The **"Spin,"** the **"Pull"** or the **"Twist."**

- To achieve **freedom of motion**, your mind must be focused on the free motion of the clubhead as you swing.

- Your senses of **feel, hearing and seeing** are all important to creating motion.

On Fine-Tuning and Troubleshooting Your Swing:

- There are **six major swing factors** that combine to produce a shot: clubhead rotation, forward-swing path, downswing angle, swing length, swing speed and smoothness.

- **You can take command of a learning situation** by teeing the ball up, shortening and slowing your swing down, and using a short-shafted/higher-lofted club. Taking command will help you fine-tune your swing or troubleshoot it when you experience a problem.

- After you've developed a good swing, your ability to keep it "in the groove" will depend on your **awareness** and your abilities to **assess** and **adjust**. Awareness is the ability to sense what is happening in your swing and what it should feel like. Assessment is the ability to detect when something is wrong. Adjustment is the ability to implement the proper change in order to remedy the problem.

On Shotmaking:

- Your ability to score well will be enhanced if you can **"paint the sky"** with many different types of shots.

- Altering the flight of a shot to make it bend or fly higher or lower is accomplished by adjusting your swing feelings and one or more of the six major swing factors.

On Recalling a Good Swing:

- To excel at golf, you have to key on **developing, remembering and duplicating** the feelings of many different shots. Such feelings are like files in a computer.

- The more you practice your ability to **recall and duplicate** different feelings, the more shots you'll be able to play and the better you'll become at performing them.

- **Visualizing the shot** you want to play is a highly effective way of recalling a good swing.

- Frequent short practice sessions will be helpful to developing and maintaining your **"feeling files."**

On Developing Better On-Course Performance:

- Your ability to perform well on the course depends on combining sound technique with a good attitude and a strong ability to focus on each individual shot.

- Your **pre-shot routine** — the pattern of steps performed before every shot — should deliver you into a state of complete focus.

- **"Steering"** the clubhead occurs when playing conditions cause mental/physical tension that hampers your ability to make a free swing.

- Playing and scoring well depends partly on your ability to manage your confidence and maintain a positive attitude.

Dean Reinmuth is a natural in the world of golf instruction. His tension-reducing methods of instruction have solved many a mystery for the tour professional and golfing enthusiast alike.

He played competitively for several years before retiring to coach others. He annually tours Japan, conducting golf schools across the country. His work with golfers has been been nothing shy of spectacular: Dean has taught Phil Mickelson since Phil was 13 years old.

Dean is a member of *Golf Digest*'s Professional Advisory Staff and was selected by *Golf* magazine as one of the top teachers in the U.S. He travels extensively, teaching, giving exhibitions, as a product spokesperson and keynote speaker. He heads his own training center and golf school at Carlton Oaks in San Diego, California, where he works with both young players and professionals as well as weekend golfers.

Sports/Golf

Relaxation + Consistency = Lower Scores

Relaxation is crucial to a good golf swing, and a relaxed and powerful swing is one of the hardest skills to master. *Tension-Free Golf* presents Dean Reinmuth's proven techniques for reducing tension– a private lesson for improving your golf swing.

"Dean Reinmuth's a great teacher. His instructional approach helped me achieve my goals, and I know he can help you achieve yours."
—*Phil Mickelson*

"A great book! Reinmuth is golf's new guru, the 'dean' of golf."
—*Dick Pressler*, President, Gant

"Dean has a very special understanding of the learning process that enables each of his students to develop their game with greater sensitivity and feel for the swing."
—*Jim Flick*, Nicklaus/Flick Golf Schools

Dean Reinmuth has earned international recognition in the golf world as a teacher and for his extensive knowledge of the game. He is a member of the *Golf Digest* instructional ad[...] commentator for the P[...]chool of golf in San Diego, a [...]hat prepares promising young amateurs and professionals for careers in competitive golf. His popular instructional video, *Take a Swing at Tension*, was given a four-star rating by *Golf* magazine and has sold more than 130,000 copies.

ISBN 1-57243-039-7

51995

9 781572 430396

TRIUMPH
B O O K S
CHICAGO